C-256 CAREER EXAMINATION SERIES

This is your
PASSBOOK for...

Fire Alarm Dispatcher

Test Preparation Study Guide
Questions & Answers

COPYRIGHT NOTICE

This book is SOLELY intended for, is sold ONLY to, and its use is RESTRICTED to individual, bona fide applicants or candidates who qualify by virtue of having seriously filed applications for appropriate license, certificate, professional and/or promotional advancement, higher school matriculation, scholarship, or other legitimate requirements of education and/or governmental authorities.

This book is NOT intended for use, class instruction, tutoring, training, duplication, copying, reprinting, excerption, or adaptation, etc., by:

1) Other publishers
2) Proprietors and/or Instructors of "Coaching" and/or Preparatory Courses
3) Personnel and/or Training Divisions of commercial, industrial, and governmental organizations
4) Schools, colleges, or universities and/or their departments and staffs, including teachers and other personnel
5) Testing Agencies or Bureaus
6) Study groups which seek by the purchase of a single volume to copy and/or duplicate and/or adapt this material for use by the group as a whole without having purchased individual volumes for each of the members of the group
7) Et al.

Such persons would be in violation of appropriate Federal and State statutes.

PROVISION OF LICENSING AGREEMENTS – Recognized educational, commercial, industrial, and governmental institutions and organizations, and others legitimately engaged in educational pursuits, including training, testing, and measurement activities, may address request for a licensing agreement to the copyright owners, who will determine whether, and under what conditions, including fees and charges, the materials in this book may be used them. In other words, a licensing facility exists for the legitimate use of the material in this book on other than an individual basis. However, it is asseverated and affirmed here that the material in this book CANNOT be used without the receipt of the express permission of such a licensing agreement from the Publishers. Inquiries re licensing should be addressed to the company, attention rights and permissions department.

All rights reserved, including the right of reproduction in whole or in part, in any form or by any means, electronic or mechanical, including photocopying, recording, or by any information storage and retrieval system, without permission in writing from the Publisher.

Copyright © 2025 by
National Learning Corporation

212 Michael Drive, Syosset, NY 11791
(516) 921-8888 • www.passbooks.com
E-mail: info@passbooks.com

PASSBOOK® SERIES

THE *PASSBOOK® SERIES* has been created to prepare applicants and candidates for the ultimate academic battlefield – the examination room.

At some time in our lives, each and every one of us may be required to take an examination – for validation, matriculation, admission, qualification, registration, certification, or licensure.

Based on the assumption that every applicant or candidate has met the basic formal educational standards, has taken the required number of courses, and read the necessary texts, the *PASSBOOK® SERIES* furnishes the one special preparation which may assure passing with confidence, instead of failing with insecurity. Examination questions – together with answers – are furnished as the basic vehicle for study so that the mysteries of the examination and its compounding difficulties may be eliminated or diminished by a sure method.

This book is meant to help you pass your examination provided that you qualify and are serious in your objective.

The entire field is reviewed through the huge store of content information which is succinctly presented through a provocative and challenging approach – the question-and-answer method.

A climate of success is established by furnishing the correct answers at the end of each test.

You soon learn to recognize types of questions, forms of questions, and patterns of questioning. You may even begin to anticipate expected outcomes.

You perceive that many questions are repeated or adapted so that you can gain acute insights, which may enable you to score many sure points.

You learn how to confront new questions, or types of questions, and to attack them confidently and work out the correct answers.

You note objectives and emphases, and recognize pitfalls and dangers, so that you may make positive educational adjustments.

Moreover, you are kept fully informed in relation to new concepts, methods, practices, and directions in the field.

You discover that you are actually taking the examination all the time: you are preparing for the examination by "taking" an examination, not by reading extraneous and/or supererogatory textbooks.

In short, this PASSBOOK®, used directedly, should be an important factor in helping you to pass your test.

FIRE ALARM DISPATCHER

DUTIES AND RESPONSIBILITIES:
　　Under direct supervision, receives and traumas alarms of fire and emergency by telephone and department facilities including voice alarm, telephone, emergency reporting system and two-way radio; performs related work.

EXAMPLES OF TYPICAL TASKS:
　　Receives coded and voice fire alarm box signals. Receives and makes recordings of all alarm activity in central office; interrogates alarm callers to elicit appropriate information. Checks alarm source and accuracy; sends standard telegraph signals to dispatch fire apparatus; dispatches fire apparatus using voice alarms and telephone systems. Varies dispatch according to location of apparatus at any given alarm and evaluates data from manually maintained information systems and computer recommendations concerning relocations, responses and interchanges of apparatus and personnel as directed by the supervising dispatcher of the tour of duty. Receives and retransmits, ordinarily by two-way radio, additional orders, requests and information, and maintains communications with fire apparatus in the field. Operates radiotelephone transmitter as required. During his tour of duty tests operability of electrical circuits and assists maintainers in tests for locating equipment faults. Employs alternative wire and power facilities to change office circuits and equipment as required. Makes records of all communications, alarms, fire apparatus responses and signal equipment maintenance actions. Employs telephonic communications to other forces in the community affected in fire and emergency situations. Prepares computer to receive and process data and enters data into computer system.

SUBJECT OF EXAMINATION:
The written test is designed to evaluate knowledge, skills and /or abilities in the following areas:
1. **Coding/decoding information** - These questions test for the ability to follow a set of coding rules. Some questions will require you to code information by converting certain information into letters or numbers. Other questions will require you to decode information by determining if the information that has already been converted into letters or numbers is correct. Complete directions will be provided; no previous knowledge of or training in any coding system is required.
2. **Following directions (maps)** - These questions test your ability to follow physical/geographic directions using street maps or building maps. You will have to read and understand a set of directions and then use them on a simple map.
3. **Retaining and comprehending spoken information from calls for emergency services** - These questions test for your ability to retain specific information that is heard in calls for emergency service, such as a street address, or to comprehend spoken information from emergency service calls, such as determining the location of a site in relation to landmarks.
4. **Radio operations and dispatching procedures** - These questions test for knowledge of two-way radio systems and operations, and may cover dispatching procedures when appropriate.
5. **Understanding and interpreting written material** - These questions test how well you comprehend written material. You will be provided with brief reading selections and will be asked questions about the selections. All the information required to answer the questions will be presented in the selections; you will not be required to have any special knowledge relating to the subject areas of the selections.

HOW TO TAKE A TEST

I. YOU MUST PASS AN EXAMINATION

A. WHAT EVERY CANDIDATE SHOULD KNOW

Examination applicants often ask us for help in preparing for the written test. What can I study in advance? What kinds of questions will be asked? How will the test be given? How will the papers be graded?

As an applicant for a civil service examination, you may be wondering about some of these things. Our purpose here is to suggest effective methods of advance study and to describe civil service examinations.

Your chances for success on this examination can be increased if you know how to prepare. Those "pre-examination jitters" can be reduced if you know what to expect. You can even experience an adventure in good citizenship if you know why civil service exams are given.

B. WHY ARE CIVIL SERVICE EXAMINATIONS GIVEN?

Civil service examinations are important to you in two ways. As a citizen, you want public jobs filled by employees who know how to do their work. As a job seeker, you want a fair chance to compete for that job on an equal footing with other candidates. The best-known means of accomplishing this two-fold goal is the competitive examination.

Exams are widely publicized throughout the nation. They may be administered for jobs in federal, state, city, municipal, town or village governments or agencies.

Any citizen may apply, with some limitations, such as the age or residence of applicants. Your experience and education may be reviewed to see whether you meet the requirements for the particular examination. When these requirements exist, they are reasonable and applied consistently to all applicants. Thus, a competitive examination may cause you some uneasiness now, but it is your privilege and safeguard.

C. HOW ARE CIVIL SERVICE EXAMS DEVELOPED?

Examinations are carefully written by trained technicians who are specialists in the field known as "psychological measurement," in consultation with recognized authorities in the field of work that the test will cover. These experts recommend the subject matter areas or skills to be tested; only those knowledges or skills important to your success on the job are included. The most reliable books and source materials available are used as references. Together, the experts and technicians judge the difficulty level of the questions.

Test technicians know how to phrase questions so that the problem is clearly stated. Their ethics do not permit "trick" or "catch" questions. Questions may have been tried out on sample groups, or subjected to statistical analysis, to determine their usefulness.

Written tests are often used in combination with performance tests, ratings of training and experience, and oral interviews. All of these measures combine to form the best-known means of finding the right person for the right job.

II. HOW TO PASS THE WRITTEN TEST

A. NATURE OF THE EXAMINATION

To prepare intelligently for civil service examinations, you should know how they differ from school examinations you have taken. In school you were assigned certain definite pages to read or subjects to cover. The examination questions were quite detailed and usually emphasized memory. Civil service exams, on the other hand, try to discover your present ability to perform the duties of a position, plus your potentiality to learn these duties. In other words, a civil service exam attempts to predict how successful you will be. Questions cover such a broad area that they cannot be as minute and detailed as school exam questions.

In the public service similar kinds of work, or positions, are grouped together in one "class." This process is known as *position-classification*. All the positions in a class are paid according to the salary range for that class. One class title covers all of these positions, and they are all tested by the same examination.

B. FOUR BASIC STEPS

1) Study the announcement

How, then, can you know what subjects to study? Our best answer is: "Learn as much as possible about the class of positions for which you've applied." The exam will test the knowledge, skills and abilities needed to do the work.

Your most valuable source of information about the position you want is the official exam announcement. This announcement lists the training and experience qualifications. Check these standards and apply only if you come reasonably close to meeting them.

The brief description of the position in the examination announcement offers some clues to the subjects which will be tested. Think about the job itself. Review the duties in your mind. Can you perform them, or are there some in which you are rusty? Fill in the blank spots in your preparation.

Many jurisdictions preview the written test in the exam announcement by including a section called "Knowledge and Abilities Required," "Scope of the Examination," or some similar heading. Here you will find out specifically what fields will be tested.

2) Review your own background

Once you learn in general what the position is all about, and what you need to know to do the work, ask yourself which subjects you already know fairly well and which need improvement. You may wonder whether to concentrate on improving your strong areas or on building some background in your fields of weakness. When the announcement has specified "some knowledge" or "considerable knowledge," or has used adjectives like "beginning principles of…" or "advanced … methods," you can get a clue as to the number and difficulty of questions to be asked in any given field. More questions, and hence broader coverage, would be included for those subjects which are more important in the work. Now weigh your strengths and weaknesses against the job requirements and prepare accordingly.

3) Determine the level of the position

Another way to tell how intensively you should prepare is to understand the level of the job for which you are applying. Is it the entering level? In other words, is this the position in which beginners in a field of work are hired? Or is it an intermediate or advanced level? Sometimes this is indicated by such words as "Junior" or "Senior" in the class title. Other jurisdictions use Roman numerals to designate the level – Clerk I, Clerk II, for example. The word "Supervisor" sometimes appears in the title. If the level is not indicated by the title, check the description of duties. Will you be working under very close supervision, or will you have responsibility for independent decisions in this work?

4) Choose appropriate study materials

Now that you know the subjects to be examined and the relative amount of each subject to be covered, you can choose suitable study materials. For beginning level jobs, or even advanced ones, if you have a pronounced weakness in some aspect of your training, read a modern, standard textbook in that field. Be sure it is up to date and has general coverage. Such books are normally available at your library, and the librarian will be glad to help you locate one. For entry-level positions, questions of appropriate difficulty are chosen – neither highly advanced questions, nor those too simple. Such questions require careful thought but not advanced training.

If the position for which you are applying is technical or advanced, you will read more advanced, specialized material. If you are already familiar with the basic principles of your field, elementary textbooks would waste your time. Concentrate on advanced textbooks and technical periodicals. Think through the concepts and review difficult problems in your field.

These are all general sources. You can get more ideas on your own initiative, following these leads. For example, training manuals and publications of the government agency which employs workers in your field can be useful, particularly for technical and professional positions. A letter or visit to the government department involved may result in more specific study suggestions, and certainly will provide you with a more definite idea of the exact nature of the position you are seeking.

III. KINDS OF TESTS

Tests are used for purposes other than measuring knowledge and ability to perform specified duties. For some positions, it is equally important to test ability to make adjustments to new situations or to profit from training. In others, basic mental abilities not dependent on information are essential. Questions which test these things may not appear as pertinent to the duties of the position as those which test for knowledge and information. Yet they are often highly important parts of a fair examination. For very general questions, it is almost impossible to help you direct your study efforts. What we can do is to point out some of the more common of these general abilities needed in public service positions and describe some typical questions.

1) General information

Broad, general information has been found useful for predicting job success in some kinds of work. This is tested in a variety of ways, from vocabulary lists to questions about current events. Basic background in some field of work, such as sociology or economics, may be sampled in a group of questions. Often these are principles which have become familiar to most persons through exposure rather than through formal training. It is difficult to advise you how to study for these questions; being alert to the world around you is our best suggestion.

2) Verbal ability

An example of an ability needed in many positions is verbal or language ability. Verbal ability is, in brief, the ability to use and understand words. Vocabulary and grammar tests are typical measures of this ability. Reading comprehension or paragraph interpretation questions are common in many kinds of civil service tests. You are given a paragraph of written material and asked to find its central meaning.

3) Numerical ability

Number skills can be tested by the familiar arithmetic problem, by checking paired lists of numbers to see which are alike and which are different, or by interpreting charts and graphs. In the latter test, a graph may be printed in the test booklet which you are asked to use as the basis for answering questions.

4) Observation

A popular test for law-enforcement positions is the observation test. A picture is shown to you for several minutes, then taken away. Questions about the picture test your ability to observe both details and larger elements.

5) Following directions

In many positions in the public service, the employee must be able to carry out written instructions dependably and accurately. You may be given a chart with several columns, each column listing a variety of information. The questions require you to carry out directions involving the information given in the chart.

6) Skills and aptitudes

Performance tests effectively measure some manual skills and aptitudes. When the skill is one in which you are trained, such as typing or shorthand, you can practice. These tests are often very much like those given in business school or high school courses. For many of the other skills and aptitudes, however, no short-time preparation can be made. Skills and abilities natural to you or that you have developed throughout your lifetime are being tested.

Many of the general questions just described provide all the data needed to answer the questions and ask you to use your reasoning ability to find the answers. Your best preparation for these tests, as well as for tests of facts and ideas, is to be at your physical and mental best. You, no doubt, have your own methods of getting into an exam-taking mood and keeping "in shape." The next section lists some ideas on this subject.

IV. KINDS OF QUESTIONS

Only rarely is the "essay" question, which you answer in narrative form, used in civil service tests. Civil service tests are usually of the short-answer type. Full instructions for answering these questions will be given to you at the examination. But in case this is your first experience with short-answer questions and separate answer sheets, here is what you need to know:

1) Multiple-choice Questions

Most popular of the short-answer questions is the "multiple choice" or "best answer" question. It can be used, for example, to test for factual knowledge, ability to solve problems or judgment in meeting situations found at work.

A multiple-choice question is normally one of three types—
- It can begin with an incomplete statement followed by several possible endings. You are to find the one ending which *best* completes the statement, although some of the others may not be entirely wrong.
- It can also be a complete statement in the form of a question which is answered by choosing one of the statements listed.

- It can be in the form of a problem – again you select the best answer.

Here is an example of a multiple-choice question with a discussion which should give you some clues as to the method for choosing the right answer:

When an employee has a complaint about his assignment, the action which will *best* help him overcome his difficulty is to
- A. discuss his difficulty with his coworkers
- B. take the problem to the head of the organization
- C. take the problem to the person who gave him the assignment
- D. say nothing to anyone about his complaint

In answering this question, you should study each of the choices to find which is best. Consider choice "A" – Certainly an employee may discuss his complaint with fellow employees, but no change or improvement can result, and the complaint remains unresolved. Choice "B" is a poor choice since the head of the organization probably does not know what assignment you have been given, and taking your problem to him is known as "going over the head" of the supervisor. The supervisor, or person who made the assignment, is the person who can clarify it or correct any injustice. Choice "C" is, therefore, correct. To say nothing, as in choice "D," is unwise. Supervisors have and interest in knowing the problems employees are facing, and the employee is seeking a solution to his problem.

2) True/False Questions

The "true/false" or "right/wrong" form of question is sometimes used. Here a complete statement is given. Your job is to decide whether the statement is right or wrong.

SAMPLE: A roaming cell-phone call to a nearby city costs less than a non-roaming call to a distant city.

This statement is wrong, or false, since roaming calls are more expensive.

This is not a complete list of all possible question forms, although most of the others are variations of these common types. You will always get complete directions for answering questions. Be sure you understand *how* to mark your answers – ask questions until you do.

V. RECORDING YOUR ANSWERS

Computer terminals are used more and more today for many different kinds of exams.

For an examination with very few applicants, you may be told to record your answers in the test booklet itself. Separate answer sheets are much more common. If this separate answer sheet is to be scored by machine – and this is often the case – it is highly important that you mark your answers correctly in order to get credit.

An electronic scoring machine is often used in civil service offices because of the speed with which papers can be scored. Machine-scored answer sheets must be marked with a pencil, which will be given to you. This pencil has a high graphite content which responds to the electronic scoring machine. As a matter of fact, stray dots may register as answers, so do not let your pencil rest on the answer sheet while you are pondering the correct answer. Also, if your pencil lead breaks or is otherwise defective, ask for another.

Since the answer sheet will be dropped in a slot in the scoring machine, be careful not to bend the corners or get the paper crumpled.

The answer sheet normally has five vertical columns of numbers, with 30 numbers to a column. These numbers correspond to the question numbers in your test booklet. After each number, going across the page are four or five pairs of dotted lines. These short dotted lines have small letters or numbers above them. The first two pairs may also have a "T" or "F" above the letters. This indicates that the first two pairs only are to be used if the questions are of the true-false type. If the questions are multiple choice, disregard the "T" and "F" and pay attention only to the small letters or numbers.

Answer your questions in the manner of the sample that follows:

32. The largest city in the United States is
    A. Washington, D.C.
    B. New York City
    C. Chicago
    D. Detroit
    E. San Francisco

1) Choose the answer you think is best. (New York City is the largest, so "B" is correct.)
2) Find the row of dotted lines numbered the same as the question you are answering. (Find row number 32)
3) Find the pair of dotted lines corresponding to the answer. (Find the pair of lines under the mark "B.")
4) Make a solid black mark between the dotted lines.

VI. BEFORE THE TEST

Common sense will help you find procedures to follow to get ready for an examination. Too many of us, however, overlook these sensible measures. Indeed, nervousness and fatigue have been found to be the most serious reasons why applicants fail to do their best on civil service tests. Here is a list of reminders:

- Begin your preparation early – Don't wait until the last minute to go scurrying around for books and materials or to find out what the position is all about.
- Prepare continuously – An hour a night for a week is better than an all-night cram session. This has been definitely established. What is more, a night a week for a month will return better dividends than crowding your study into a shorter period of time.
- Locate the place of the exam – You have been sent a notice telling you when and where to report for the examination. If the location is in a different town or otherwise unfamiliar to you, it would be well to inquire the best route and learn something about the building.
- Relax the night before the test – Allow your mind to rest. Do not study at all that night. Plan some mild recreation or diversion; then go to bed early and get a good night's sleep.
- Get up early enough to make a leisurely trip to the place for the test – This way unforeseen events, traffic snarls, unfamiliar buildings, etc. will not upset you.
- Dress comfortably – A written test is not a fashion show. You will be known by number and not by name, so wear something comfortable.

- Leave excess paraphernalia at home – Shopping bags and odd bundles will get in your way. You need bring only the items mentioned in the official notice you received; usually everything you need is provided. Do not bring reference books to the exam. They will only confuse those last minutes and be taken away from you when in the test room.
- Arrive somewhat ahead of time – If because of transportation schedules you must get there very early, bring a newspaper or magazine to take your mind off yourself while waiting.
- Locate the examination room – When you have found the proper room, you will be directed to the seat or part of the room where you will sit. Sometimes you are given a sheet of instructions to read while you are waiting. Do not fill out any forms until you are told to do so; just read them and be prepared.
- Relax and prepare to listen to the instructions
- If you have any physical problem that may keep you from doing your best, be sure to tell the test administrator. If you are sick or in poor health, you really cannot do your best on the exam. You can come back and take the test some other time.

VII. AT THE TEST

The day of the test is here and you have the test booklet in your hand. The temptation to get going is very strong. Caution! There is more to success than knowing the right answers. You must know how to identify your papers and understand variations in the type of short-answer question used in this particular examination. Follow these suggestions for maximum results from your efforts:

1) Cooperate with the monitor

The test administrator has a duty to create a situation in which you can be as much at ease as possible. He will give instructions, tell you when to begin, check to see that you are marking your answer sheet correctly, and so on. He is not there to guard you, although he will see that your competitors do not take unfair advantage. He wants to help you do your best.

2) Listen to all instructions

Don't jump the gun! Wait until you understand all directions. In most civil service tests you get more time than you need to answer the questions. So don't be in a hurry. Read each word of instructions until you clearly understand the meaning. Study the examples, listen to all announcements and follow directions. Ask questions if you do not understand what to do.

3) Identify your papers

Civil service exams are usually identified by number only. You will be assigned a number; you must not put your name on your test papers. Be sure to copy your number correctly. Since more than one exam may be given, copy your exact examination title.

4) Plan your time

Unless you are told that a test is a "speed" or "rate of work" test, speed itself is usually not important. Time enough to answer all the questions will be provided, but this does not mean that you have all day. An overall time limit has been set. Divide the total time (in minutes) by the number of questions to determine the approximate time you have for each question.

5) Do not linger over difficult questions

If you come across a difficult question, mark it with a paper clip (useful to have along) and come back to it when you have been through the booklet. One caution if you do this – be sure to skip a number on your answer sheet as well. Check often to be sure that you have not lost your place and that you are marking in the row numbered the same as the question you are answering.

6) Read the questions

Be sure you know what the question asks! Many capable people are unsuccessful because they failed to *read* the questions correctly.

7) Answer all questions

Unless you have been instructed that a penalty will be deducted for incorrect answers, it is better to guess than to omit a question.

8) Speed tests

It is often better NOT to guess on speed tests. It has been found that on timed tests people are tempted to spend the last few seconds before time is called in marking answers at random – without even reading them – in the hope of picking up a few extra points. To discourage this practice, the instructions may warn you that your score will be "corrected" for guessing. That is, a penalty will be applied. The incorrect answers will be deducted from the correct ones, or some other penalty formula will be used.

9) Review your answers

If you finish before time is called, go back to the questions you guessed or omitted to give them further thought. Review other answers if you have time.

10) Return your test materials

If you are ready to leave before others have finished or time is called, take ALL your materials to the monitor and leave quietly. Never take any test material with you. The monitor can discover whose papers are not complete, and taking a test booklet may be grounds for disqualification.

VIII. EXAMINATION TECHNIQUES

1) Read the general instructions carefully. These are usually printed on the first page of the exam booklet. As a rule, these instructions refer to the timing of the examination; the fact that you should not start work until the signal and must stop work at a signal, etc. If there are any *special* instructions, such as a choice of questions to be answered, make sure that you note this instruction carefully.

2) When you are ready to start work on the examination, that is as soon as the signal has been given, read the instructions to each question booklet, underline any key words or phrases, such as *least, best, outline, describe* and the like. In this way you will tend to answer as requested rather than discover on reviewing your paper that you *listed without describing*, that you selected the *worst* choice rather than the *best* choice, etc.

3) If the examination is of the objective or multiple-choice type – that is, each question will also give a series of possible answers: A, B, C or D, and you are called upon to select the best answer and write the letter next to that answer on your answer paper – it is advisable to start answering each question in turn. There may be anywhere from 50 to 100 such questions in the three or four hours allotted and you can see how much time would be taken if you read through all the questions before beginning to answer any. Furthermore, if you come across a question or group of questions which you know would be difficult to answer, it would undoubtedly affect your handling of all the other questions.

4) If the examination is of the essay type and contains but a few questions, it is a moot point as to whether you should read all the questions before starting to answer any one. Of course, if you are given a choice – say five out of seven and the like – then it is essential to read all the questions so you can eliminate the two that are most difficult. If, however, you are asked to answer all the questions, there may be danger in trying to answer the easiest one first because you may find that you will spend too much time on it. The best technique is to answer the first question, then proceed to the second, etc.

5) Time your answers. Before the exam begins, write down the time it started, then add the time allowed for the examination and write down the time it must be completed, then divide the time available somewhat as follows:
    - If 3-1/2 hours are allowed, that would be 210 minutes. If you have 80 objective-type questions, that would be an average of 2-1/2 minutes per question. Allow yourself no more than 2 minutes per question, or a total of 160 minutes, which will permit about 50 minutes to review.
    - If for the time allotment of 210 minutes there are 7 essay questions to answer, that would average about 30 minutes a question. Give yourself only 25 minutes per question so that you have about 35 minutes to review.

6) The most important instruction is to *read each question* and make sure you know what is wanted. The second most important instruction is to *time yourself properly* so that you answer every question. The third most important instruction is to *answer every question*. Guess if you have to but include something for each question. Remember that you will receive no credit for a blank and will probably receive some credit if you write something in answer to an essay question. If you guess a letter – say "B" for a multiple-choice question – you may have guessed right. If you leave a blank as an answer to a multiple-choice question, the examiners may respect your feelings but it will not add a point to your score. Some exams may penalize you for wrong answers, so in such cases *only*, you may not want to guess unless you have some basis for your answer.

7) Suggestions
    a. Objective-type questions
        1. Examine the question booklet for proper sequence of pages and questions
        2. Read all instructions carefully
        3. Skip any question which seems too difficult; return to it after all other questions have been answered
        4. Apportion your time properly; do not spend too much time on any single question or group of questions

5. Note and underline key words – *all, most, fewest, least, best, worst, same, opposite,* etc.
6. Pay particular attention to negatives
7. Note unusual option, e.g., unduly long, short, complex, different or similar in content to the body of the question
8. Observe the use of "hedging" words – *probably, may, most likely,* etc.
9. Make sure that your answer is put next to the same number as the question
10. Do not second-guess unless you have good reason to believe the second answer is definitely more correct
11. Cross out original answer if you decide another answer is more accurate; do not erase until you are ready to hand your paper in
12. Answer all questions; guess unless instructed otherwise
13. Leave time for review

b. Essay questions
 1. Read each question carefully
 2. Determine exactly what is wanted. Underline key words or phrases.
 3. Decide on outline or paragraph answer
 4. Include many different points and elements unless asked to develop any one or two points or elements
 5. Show impartiality by giving pros and cons unless directed to select one side only
 6. Make and write down any assumptions you find necessary to answer the questions
 7. Watch your English, grammar, punctuation and choice of words
 8. Time your answers; don't crowd material

8) Answering the essay question

Most essay questions can be answered by framing the specific response around several key words or ideas. Here are a few such key words or ideas:

M's: manpower, materials, methods, money, management
P's: purpose, program, policy, plan, procedure, practice, problems, pitfalls, personnel, public relations

 a. Six basic steps in handling problems:
  1. Preliminary plan and background development
  2. Collect information, data and facts
  3. Analyze and interpret information, data and facts
  4. Analyze and develop solutions as well as make recommendations
  5. Prepare report and sell recommendations
  6. Install recommendations and follow up effectiveness

 b. Pitfalls to avoid
  1. *Taking things for granted* – A statement of the situation does not necessarily imply that each of the elements is necessarily true; for example, a complaint may be invalid and biased so that all that can be taken for granted is that a complaint has been registered

2. *Considering only one side of a situation* – Wherever possible, indicate several alternatives and then point out the reasons you selected the best one
3. *Failing to indicate follow up* – Whenever your answer indicates action on your part, make certain that you will take proper follow-up action to see how successful your recommendations, procedures or actions turn out to be
4. *Taking too long in answering any single question* – Remember to time your answers properly

IX. AFTER THE TEST

Scoring procedures differ in detail among civil service jurisdictions although the general principles are the same. Whether the papers are hand-scored or graded by machine we have described, they are nearly always graded by number. That is, the person who marks the paper knows only the number – never the name – of the applicant. Not until all the papers have been graded will they be matched with names. If other tests, such as training and experience or oral interview ratings have been given, scores will be combined. Different parts of the examination usually have different weights. For example, the written test might count 60 percent of the final grade, and a rating of training and experience 40 percent. In many jurisdictions, veterans will have a certain number of points added to their grades.

After the final grade has been determined, the names are placed in grade order and an eligible list is established. There are various methods for resolving ties between those who get the same final grade – probably the most common is to place first the name of the person whose application was received first. Job offers are made from the eligible list in the order the names appear on it. You will be notified of your grade and your rank as soon as all these computations have been made. This will be done as rapidly as possible.

People who are found to meet the requirements in the announcement are called "eligibles." Their names are put on a list of eligible candidates. An eligible's chances of getting a job depend on how high he stands on this list and how fast agencies are filling jobs from the list.

When a job is to be filled from a list of eligibles, the agency asks for the names of people on the list of eligibles for that job. When the civil service commission receives this request, it sends to the agency the names of the three people highest on this list. Or, if the job to be filled has specialized requirements, the office sends the agency the names of the top three persons who meet these requirements from the general list.

The appointing officer makes a choice from among the three people whose names were sent to him. If the selected person accepts the appointment, the names of the others are put back on the list to be considered for future openings.

That is the rule in hiring from all kinds of eligible lists, whether they are for typist, carpenter, chemist, or something else. For every vacancy, the appointing officer has his choice of any one of the top three eligibles on the list. This explains why the person whose name is on top of the list sometimes does not get an appointment when some of the persons lower on the list do. If the appointing officer chooses the second or third eligible, the No. 1 eligible does not get a job at once, but stays on the list until he is appointed or the list is terminated.

X. HOW TO PASS THE INTERVIEW TEST

The examination for which you applied requires an oral interview test. You have already taken the written test and you are now being called for the interview test – the final part of the formal examination.

You may think that it is not possible to prepare for an interview test and that there are no procedures to follow during an interview. Our purpose is to point out some things you can do in advance that will help you and some good rules to follow and pitfalls to avoid while you are being interviewed.

What is an interview supposed to test?

The written examination is designed to test the technical knowledge and competence of the candidate; the oral is designed to evaluate intangible qualities, not readily measured otherwise, and to establish a list showing the relative fitness of each candidate – as measured against his competitors – for the position sought. Scoring is not on the basis of "right" and "wrong," but on a sliding scale of values ranging from "not passable" to "outstanding." As a matter of fact, it is possible to achieve a relatively low score without a single "incorrect" answer because of evident weakness in the qualities being measured.

Occasionally, an examination may consist entirely of an oral test – either an individual or a group oral. In such cases, information is sought concerning the technical knowledges and abilities of the candidate, since there has been no written examination for this purpose. More commonly, however, an oral test is used to supplement a written examination.

Who conducts interviews?

The composition of oral boards varies among different jurisdictions. In nearly all, a representative of the personnel department serves as chairman. One of the members of the board may be a representative of the department in which the candidate would work. In some cases, "outside experts" are used, and, frequently, a businessman or some other representative of the general public is asked to serve. Labor and management or other special groups may be represented. The aim is to secure the services of experts in the appropriate field.

However the board is composed, it is a good idea (and not at all improper or unethical) to ascertain in advance of the interview who the members are and what groups they represent. When you are introduced to them, you will have some idea of their backgrounds and interests, and at least you will not stutter and stammer over their names.

What should be done before the interview?

While knowledge about the board members is useful and takes some of the surprise element out of the interview, there is other preparation which is more substantive. It *is* possible to prepare for an oral interview – in several ways:

1) Keep a copy of your application and review it carefully before the interview

This may be the only document before the oral board, and the starting point of the interview. Know what education and experience you have listed there, and the sequence and dates of all of it. Sometimes the board will ask you to review the highlights of your experience for them; you should not have to hem and haw doing it.

2) Study the class specification and the examination announcement

Usually, the oral board has one or both of these to guide them. The qualities, characteristics or knowledges required by the position sought are stated in these documents. They offer valuable clues as to the nature of the oral interview. For example, if the job involves supervisory responsibilities, the announcement will usually indicate that knowledge of modern supervisory methods and the qualifications of the candidate as a supervisor will be tested. If so, you can expect such questions, frequently in the form of a hypothetical situation which you are expected to solve. NEVER go into an oral without knowledge of the duties and responsibilities of the job you seek.

3) Think through each qualification required

Try to visualize the kind of questions you would ask if you were a board member. How well could you answer them? Try especially to appraise your own knowledge and background in each area, *measured against the job sought*, and identify any areas in which you are weak. Be critical and realistic – do not flatter yourself.

4) Do some general reading in areas in which you feel you may be weak

For example, if the job involves supervision and your past experience has NOT, some general reading in supervisory methods and practices, particularly in the field of human relations, might be useful. Do NOT study agency procedures or detailed manuals. The oral board will be testing your understanding and capacity, not your memory.

5) Get a good night's sleep and watch your general health and mental attitude

You will want a clear head at the interview. Take care of a cold or any other minor ailment, and of course, no hangovers.

What should be done on the day of the interview?

Now comes the day of the interview itself. Give yourself plenty of time to get there. Plan to arrive somewhat ahead of the scheduled time, particularly if your appointment is in the fore part of the day. If a previous candidate fails to appear, the board might be ready for you a bit early. By early afternoon an oral board is almost invariably behind schedule if there are many candidates, and you may have to wait. Take along a book or magazine to read, or your application to review, but leave any extraneous material in the waiting room when you go in for your interview. In any event, relax and compose yourself.

The matter of dress is important. The board is forming impressions about you – from your experience, your manners, your attitude, and your appearance. Give your personal appearance careful attention. Dress your best, but not your flashiest. Choose conservative, appropriate clothing, and be sure it is immaculate. This is a business interview, and your appearance should indicate that you regard it as such. Besides, being well groomed and properly dressed will help boost your confidence.

Sooner or later, someone will call your name and escort you into the interview room. *This is it.* From here on you are on your own. It is too late for any more preparation. But remember, you asked for this opportunity to prove your fitness, and you are here because your request was granted.

What happens when you go in?

The usual sequence of events will be as follows: The clerk (who is often the board stenographer) will introduce you to the chairman of the oral board, who will introduce you to the other members of the board. Acknowledge the introductions before you sit down. Do not be surprised if you find a microphone facing you or a stenotypist sitting by. Oral interviews are usually recorded in the event of an appeal or other review.

Usually the chairman of the board will open the interview by reviewing the highlights of your education and work experience from your application – primarily for the benefit of the other members of the board, as well as to get the material into the record. Do not interrupt or comment unless there is an error or significant misinterpretation; if that is the case, do not hesitate. But do not quibble about insignificant matters. Also, he will usually ask you some question about your education, experience or your present job – partly to get you to start talking and to establish the interviewing "rapport." He may start the actual questioning, or turn it over to one of the other members. Frequently, each member undertakes the questioning on a particular area, one in which he is perhaps most competent, so you can expect each member to participate in the examination. Because time is limited, you may also expect some rather abrupt switches in the direction the questioning takes, so do not be upset by it. Normally, a board member will not pursue a single line of questioning unless he discovers a particular strength or weakness.

After each member has participated, the chairman will usually ask whether any member has any further questions, then will ask you if you have anything you wish to add. Unless you are expecting this question, it may floor you. Worse, it may start you off on an extended, extemporaneous speech. The board is not usually seeking more information. The question is principally to offer you a last opportunity to present further qualifications or to indicate that you have nothing to add. So, if you feel that a significant qualification or characteristic has been overlooked, it is proper to point it out in a sentence or so. Do not compliment the board on the thoroughness of their examination – they have been sketchy, and you know it. If you wish, merely say, "No thank you, I have nothing further to add." This is a point where you can "talk yourself out" of a good impression or fail to present an important bit of information. Remember, *you close the interview yourself*.

The chairman will then say, "That is all, Mr. _____, thank you." Do not be startled; the interview is over, and quicker than you think. Thank him, gather your belongings and take your leave. Save your sigh of relief for the other side of the door.

How to put your best foot forward

Throughout this entire process, you may feel that the board individually and collectively is trying to pierce your defenses, seek out your hidden weaknesses and embarrass and confuse you. Actually, this is not true. They are obliged to make an appraisal of your qualifications for the job you are seeking, and they want to see you in your best light. Remember, they must interview all candidates and a non-cooperative candidate may become a failure in spite of their best efforts to bring out his qualifications. Here are 15 suggestions that will help you:

1) **Be natural – Keep your attitude confident, not cocky**

If you are not confident that you can do the job, do not expect the board to be. Do not apologize for your weaknesses, try to bring out your strong points. The board is interested in a positive, not negative, presentation. Cockiness will antagonize any board member and make him wonder if you are covering up a weakness by a false show of strength.

2) **Get comfortable, but don't lounge or sprawl**

Sit erectly but not stiffly. A careless posture may lead the board to conclude that you are careless in other things, or at least that you are not impressed by the importance of the occasion. Either conclusion is natural, even if incorrect. Do not fuss with your clothing, a pencil or an ashtray. Your hands may occasionally be useful to emphasize a point; do not let them become a point of distraction.

3) **Do not wisecrack or make small talk**

This is a serious situation, and your attitude should show that you consider it as such. Further, the time of the board is limited – they do not want to waste it, and neither should you.

4) Do not exaggerate your experience or abilities

In the first place, from information in the application or other interviews and sources, the board may know more about you than you think. Secondly, you probably will not get away with it. An experienced board is rather adept at spotting such a situation, so do not take the chance.

5) If you know a board member, do not make a point of it, yet do not hide it

Certainly you are not fooling him, and probably not the other members of the board. Do not try to take advantage of your acquaintanceship – it will probably do you little good.

6) Do not dominate the interview

Let the board do that. They will give you the clues – do not assume that you have to do all the talking. Realize that the board has a number of questions to ask you, and do not try to take up all the interview time by showing off your extensive knowledge of the answer to the first one.

7) Be attentive

You only have 20 minutes or so, and you should keep your attention at its sharpest throughout. When a member is addressing a problem or question to you, give him your undivided attention. Address your reply principally to him, but do not exclude the other board members.

8) Do not interrupt

A board member may be stating a problem for you to analyze. He will ask you a question when the time comes. Let him state the problem, and wait for the question.

9) Make sure you understand the question

Do not try to answer until you are sure what the question is. If it is not clear, restate it in your own words or ask the board member to clarify it for you. However, do not haggle about minor elements.

10) Reply promptly but not hastily

A common entry on oral board rating sheets is "candidate responded readily," or "candidate hesitated in replies." Respond as promptly and quickly as you can, but do not jump to a hasty, ill-considered answer.

11) Do not be peremptory in your answers

A brief answer is proper – but do not fire your answer back. That is a losing game from your point of view. The board member can probably ask questions much faster than you can answer them.

12) Do not try to create the answer you think the board member wants

He is interested in what kind of mind you have and how it works – not in playing games. Furthermore, he can usually spot this practice and will actually grade you down on it.

13) Do not switch sides in your reply merely to agree with a board member

Frequently, a member will take a contrary position merely to draw you out and to see if you are willing and able to defend your point of view. Do not start a debate, yet do not surrender a good position. If a position is worth taking, it is worth defending.

14) Do not be afraid to admit an error in judgment if you are shown to be wrong

The board knows that you are forced to reply without any opportunity for careful consideration. Your answer may be demonstrably wrong. If so, admit it and get on with the interview.

15) Do not dwell at length on your present job

The opening question may relate to your present assignment. Answer the question but do not go into an extended discussion. You are being examined for a *new* job, not your present one. As a matter of fact, try to phrase ALL your answers in terms of the job for which you are being examined.

Basis of Rating

Probably you will forget most of these "do's" and "don'ts" when you walk into the oral interview room. Even remembering them all will not ensure you a passing grade. Perhaps you did not have the qualifications in the first place. But remembering them will help you to put your best foot forward, without treading on the toes of the board members.

Rumor and popular opinion to the contrary notwithstanding, an oral board wants you to make the best appearance possible. They know you are under pressure – but they also want to see how you respond to it as a guide to what your reaction would be under the pressures of the job you seek. They will be influenced by the degree of poise you display, the personal traits you show and the manner in which you respond.

ABOUT THIS BOOK

This book contains tests divided into Examination Sections. Go through each test, answering every question in the margin. We have also attached a sample answer sheet at the back of the book that can be removed and used. At the end of each test look at the answer key and check your answers. On the ones you got wrong, look at the right answer choice and learn. Do not fill in the answers first. Do not memorize the questions and answers, but understand the answer and principles involved. On your test, the questions will likely be different from the samples. Questions are changed and new ones added. If you understand these past questions you should have success with any changes that arise. Tests may consist of several types of questions. We have additional books on each subject should more study be advisable or necessary for you. Finally, the more you study, the better prepared you will be. This book is intended to be the last thing you study before you walk into the examination room. Prior study of relevant texts is also recommended. NLC publishes some of these in our Fundamental Series. Knowledge and good sense are important factors in passing your exam. Good luck also helps. So now study this Passbook, absorb the material contained within and take that knowledge into the examination. Then do your best to pass that exam.

EXAMINATION SECTION

EXAMINATION SECTION
TEST 1

DIRECTIONS: Each question or incomplete statement is followed by several suggested answers or completions. Select the one that BEST answers the question or completes the statement. *PRINT THE LETTER OF THE CORRECT ANSWER IN THE SPACE AT THE RIGHT.*

1. Alarms of fire reported by telephone are recorded. The BEST reason for such a practice is to

    A. determine the number of calls from foreign language callers
    B. indicate the time of alarm so that any delays in telephone company facilities can be noted
    C. provide an accurate count of the number of telephone alarms received
    D. provide means for verification of the information given in the call

1.____

2. Conventional current in a circuit energized by a battery flows

    A. from the positive terminal of the battery to the negative terminal
    B. from the negative terminal of the battery to the positive terminal
    C. forward and backward, reversing direction 60 times a second
    D. in equal amounts from both positive and negative terminals of the battery to ground

2.____

3. The procedures governing radio operations by the Fire Department in the Bureau of Fire Communications are under Federal government control.
   The agency responsible for this function is

    A. Conelrad
    B. the General Services Administration
    C. the Federal Communications Commission
    D. the Department of Health, Education and Welfare

3.____

4. Radio messages concerning fires are divided into two general classifications, urgent and routine.
   The one of the following which would NOT be considered urgent is

    A. notification that the relief personnel are to report to the fire location at tour change
    B. a unit stopping to extinguish a fire encountered on the way to another alarm
    C. a unit breaking down while responding to an alarm
    D. additional information being received by telephone that persons are believed trapped in a fire

4.____

5. In connection with fires, a summary report must be submitted to higher fire authorities. The communications office is responsible for submitting this report because there is less stress in this office than at the scene of the fire. The dispatcher obtains the pertinent data from a radio contact at the fire.
   Of the following practices, the efficient dispatcher should

    A. get all the information from the radio contact at the fire, in order to provide an accurate summary of conditions at the fire
    B. permit the radio contact to postpone his report until the fire is over

5.____

1

C. tell the radio contact that fire officials are calling for information whether true or not
D. slow down the conversation to below normal so that the radio contact will have to slow down the message

6. The MOST accurate of the following statements concerning the activities of the Fire Department this year as compared to last year is:

   A. The number of fires has increased
   B. Larger fires (3rd, 4th, and 5th alarms) have increased
   C. The number of 2nd alarm fires has decreased
   D. False alarms have increased

7. The amount of electricity that can be taken from a battery is measured in

   A. kilowatts
   B. amperes
   C. watt-hours
   D. decibels

8. One reason that transistors have replaced vacuum tubes in electronic circuits is that transistors

   A. never break down
   B. are less expensive than tubes
   C. do not have filaments that have to warm up
   D. are all interchangeable with each other

9. The one of the following which would NOT ordinarily be required of a dispatcher as a routine duty is

   A. testing operability of electrical circuits and assisting maintainers in tests for locating equipment faults
   B. employing telephonic communication to other forces in the community affected in fire and emergency situations
   C. preparing duty assignments for the dispatchers in the communications office
   D. receiving coded and voice alarm box signals

10. The GREATEST overall advantage of the introduction of radio communications in the Fire Department was making possible

    A. a greatly reduced number of fire companies in the Department
    B. regular contact between units out of quarters and the communications office
    C. the elimination of telegraphic communications
    D. fire prevention field inspections with apparatus and members

11. The MOST important reason for a dispatcher to have good command of the situation in radio communication is to

    A. provide accuracy in his messages and thereby save time
    B. calm the person who is being contacted
    C. let the listener understand that the dispatcher is interested in his problem
    D. protect himself because many persons are *listening in* and may be critical

12. Notification signals are sent to other counties when a major alarm is raging in a particular county.
    The LEAST accurate of the following reasons for such notification is that

A. units from other counties may be assigned to the alarm or relocated in the county in which the fire is located
B. special units may be assigned from other counties
C. all dispatchers may be alerted to the possibility that some units which are assigned to respond to their county may not be available because of operations at the other fire
D. firefighters on off tours must be notified in the event they may be needed if conditions so demand

13. Of the following types of units, the largest number of fire companies consist of 13.____

   A. Ladder B. Engine
   C. Tower ladders D. Rescue

14. The time period during which the GREATEST number of fire alarms occur is 14.____

   A. 11 P.M. to 7 A.M. B. 7 A.M. to 3 P.M.
   C. 3 P.M. to 11 P.M. D. 3 A.M. to 11 A.M.

15. The Communications Bureau has been called the *nerve center* of the Fire Department. 15.____
The BEST explanation for this is that

   A. alarms by telegraph or voice communication are the means by which units respond to fires and emergencies
   B. all important decisions are made by this Bureau
   C. the Department as a whole is guided by this Bureau in major fire incidents
   D. decisions are made here for the field commanders

16. Some frequency modulation (FM) receivers are equipped with AFC. 16.____
AFC stands for

   A. automatic frequency control
   B. audio frequency correction
   C. amplitude fine control
   D. audio frequency compensation

17. The one of the following which is NOT considered a part of a radio dispatching system is a 17.____

   A. bell alarm receiving unit in firehouse
   B. two-way mobile unit
   C. base transmitter
   D. base station

18. When a considerable number of fire alarm boxes on a circuit are out of service because of a storm or other reason, cards are placed on the box indicating that the boxes are out of service. 18.____
Under these circumstances, if a fire should occur, people wishing to report it would be BEST advised to

   A. go to the nearest firehouse
   B. use the nearest telephone
   C. go to the nearest police station
   D. wait for a police car to pass by on patrol

Question 19.

DIRECTIONS: Question 19 is based on the following paragraph.

Fire alarm boxes are electromechanical devices for transmitting a coded signal. In each box there is a trainwork of wheels. When the box is operated, a spring-activated code wheel within begins to revolve. The code number of the box is notched on the circumference of the code wheel and the latter is associated with the circuit in such a way that when it revolves it causes the circuit to open and close in a predetermined manner, thereby transmitting its particular signal to the central station. A fire alarm box is nothing more than a device for interrupting the flow of current in a circuit in such a way as to produce a coded signal that may be decoded by the dispatchers in the central office.

19. Based on the above, select the FALSE statement.

    A. Each standard fire alarm box has its own code wheel.
    B. The code wheel operates when the box is pulled.
    C. The code wheel is operated electrically.
    D. Only the break in the circuit by the notched wheel causes the alarm signal to be transmitted to the central office.

20. If a person reporting a fire by telephone is cool and collected, is able to get an immediate connection, and speaks clearly, he will probably get a response of fire apparatus more quickly than if he traveled fifteen floors to the street and began to search for the nearest fire alarm box.
    The above statement MOST clearly indicates which of the following?

    A. Fire alarm boxes are on the way out because of the efficiency of the telephone.
    B. A telephone is always faster than use of a fire alarm box to report a fire.
    C. At times the telephone may be more advantageous in sending an alarm than a fire alarm box.
    D. Fire alarm boxes are the most dependable means of sending an alarm.

21. Knowledge of the various types of buildings is important for dispatchers because they must make decisions on number and type of equipment based in part on this factor. A building erected to house not more than two families would be classified as a

    A. tenement house
    B. converted Class A building
    C. town house
    D. dwelling

22. Among other duties, dispatchers play a role in helping prevent abuse of water hydrants causing waste of water by issuing instructions to solve the problem. Unauthorized opening of hydrants during the hot summer months wastes literally millions of gallons of water. Dispatchers receive many communications from the general public as well as from official sources concerning such unauthorized openings.
    They should know that, of the following, the one instruction that should NOT be issued to control this problem is to order

    A. a quick shutdown where hydrants are found open
    B. the issuance of spray nozzles to permit street showers

C. the installation of hydrant harnesses which are designed to make the opening and use of hydrants difficult
D. a fireman to make an immediate arrest of a person who opens a hydrant illegally

23. Of the following, the source providing the LEAST amount of water supply for the city is

   A. private wells and private water supply companies
   B. the Ashokan Reservoir
   C. the Croton System
   D. the Catskill System

24. Fire cannot exist unless there are three things present.
Of the following, the one that is NOT necessary for all combustion is

   A. an electric spark
   B. a combustible material
   C. a source of ignition, such as match, flame, etc.
   D. oxygen, usually from the air

25. An office building fire safety director makes it a practice to call the dispatcher and advise him of the date, time, and location of fire drills.
Of the following, the LEAST acceptable reason for this is to

   A. notify local chiefs in the event they desire to attend and check on the drill
   B. prevent unnecessary alarms in the event that building occupants are concerned when they hear alarm bells
   C. at drill time
   D. alert the dispatcher to the specific address of the building and the time of the fire drill for his records
   E. get credit for complying with the requirement that fire drills be held every three months

26. Fire alarms must be transmitted as quickly as possible CHIEFLY in order to

   A. get the fire apparatus on the way to the fire promptly
   B. empty the building of occupants quickly
   C. reduce fear and panic of the occupants
   D. prevent a building fire brigade from attempting to fight the fire

27. *Running time,* as applied to the response of fire apparatus, refers to

   A. plotting the distance in a straight line from the firehouse to an alarm box and applying average speed per hour
   B. an estimate of the actual time to get from firehouse to a fire
   C. a list in the firehouse of the time it takes to get to a fire alarm box under normal conditions
   D. the time taken to respond when the road traffic is lightest

28. At times the press calls the dispatcher for information on a fire or other incident.
In such a situation, a dispatcher should GENERALLY

   A. call the Chief at the location of the incident and have him call the press
   B. refer the matter to the supervising dispatcher

C. check log and give any information available
D. tell the caller that you are not allowed to give any information

29. The BEST reason for care in recording information received at a communications office is that

    A. the information is important for present and future reference
    B. it helps to reduce blame for mistakes when they are made
    C. time can be saved if the writing is legible
    D. dispatchers must follow rules at all times

29.___

30. The BEST reason for a good report and investigation of an accident to a dispatcher is to

    A. obtain proper treatment for the injury
    B. prevent the same type of accident from occurring again
    C. ascertain if the person is *accident-prone*
    D. compile accurate statistics on accidents

30.___

31. There are several types of alarm systems in buildings. The most effective are those which send an alarm to the Fire Department or a privately owned supervisory alarm service which sends the alarm received to the Fire Department.
Of the following, the one that would be the LEAST efficient in an unoccupied building would be a

    A. smoke detector   B. heat detector
    C. manual pull box   D. rate-of-rise detector

31.___

32. Standard fire alarm boxes are installed as a requirement of law in

    A. public schools   B. old-age homes
    C. nurseries   D. hospitals

32.___

33. The one of the following devices which is NOT operated by temperature controls is a

    A. sprinkler fire extinguishing system
    B. standpipe system
    C. fixed temperature unit
    D. fusible link

33.___

34. A broken water main is of particular concern to the Fire Department.
The MOST important reason for this is that

    A. loss of water can seriously handicap firefighting in an area
    B. people may be trapped in high areas of buildings by water flowing from the main
    C. apparatus may be unable to pass the flooded area
    D. street pavements could collapse and autos fall into openings

34.___

35. In former years, a certain county was relatively handicapped in firefighting because of the need to use ferries to get fire units to that county for fighting large fires. This has been resolved by

    A. doubling the number of fire companies in that county
    B. utilizing the ferry to provide additional companies from the connecting county
    C. eliminating the ferry
    D. the building of a connecting bridge

35.___

36. The PRINCIPAL reason for the installation of voice alarm boxes for reporting fires is to

    A. record the voice of the person calling in the alarm
    B. identify juvenile callers
    C. assist the dispatcher in determining what type of assignment is appropriate based on the information given
    D. guarantee that fewer false alarms will be transmitted than from standard type boxes

37. Fires are classified as accidental, suspicious, or incendiary. If a fire is declared suspicious, the dispatcher must for various reasons notify certain individuals or organizations automatically or by direction.
    Which of the following is the LEAST desirable reason for such a notification?
    To

    A. notify the press to help affected individuals in connection with any future legal action to recover economic losses
    B. alert the Fire Marshal so that an early investigation can begin
    C. make it positively known to the Chief at the fire that the fire is suspicious so that evidence will be preserved for use in the investigation by the Fire Marshal
    D. summon by radio and telephone other agencies such as Police, F.B.I., when directed by the supervising dispatcher

38. When a box is pulled and the dispatcher receives the signal, he makes the decision as to whether or not the alarm should be transmitted to the appropriate fire company because not every alarm that is received is transmitted.
    This statement MOST NEARLY refers to

    A. false alarms
    B. cases where a number of alarms are received from several boxes near a fire for which an alarm was already sent
    C. cases where no First Alarm Units are in service to respond on first alarm
    D. cases where boxes are being pulled to harass the Fire Department with rubbish fires

39. A fire alarm box must be rewound by a uniformed officer after it is rung.
    The PRINCIPAL reason is that

    A. if it is left unwound, the box may not ring when it is pulled again
    B. it is standard procedure to keep field forces alert
    C. all persons receiving the alarm will know the exact location of the box
    D. uniformed personnel will become acquainted with the type of box — pull handle or turn handle

40. The Fire Department locates its communications centers in park areas CHIEFLY because

    A. such locations provide security for the communications center from fire possibilities in a built-up area
    B. the fire alarm cables are more accessible than if surrounded by buildings
    C. there is adequate parking for emergency repair vehicles
    D. the environment is more pleasant for dispatcher crews

41. In addition to voice alarm, radio, and telephone, another component of the communications system for fire protection is

    A. television
    B. semaphore
    C. phonics
    D. telegraph

42. A voltmeter will give the most accurate reading when the range selected is such that the pointer settles at the

    A. upper end of the scale
    B. middle region of the scale
    C. lower end of the scale
    D. same position on the scale when the leads are reversed

43. A 10-to-1 step-down transformer has an input of 1 ampere at 110 volts A.C. If the losses are negligible, the output of the transformer is _____ ampere(s) at _____ volts.

    A. 1; 12   B. 10; 12   C. 1; 1200   D. 10; 120

44. If a test lamp lights when placed directly across a fuse, it should be concluded that

    A. the fuse is good
    B. the fuse is over-rated
    C. the fuse is blown
    D. further tests are required to determine the condition of the fuse

45. A circular mil is a measure of electrical conductor

    A. length
    B. cross-section area
    C. volume
    D. weight

46. A shunt is a device that is part of a(n)

    A. voltmeter
    B. ammeter
    C. inductor
    D. capacitor

47. The amplitude of a transmitted signal at a distance from the transmitter can be measured by means of a

    A. Beat-Frequency Oscillator
    B. Q-Meter
    C. Field Strength Meter
    D. Discriminator

48. *Dipole* is a word used to describe a certain type of

    A. antenna
    B. transistor
    C. battery
    D. insulation

49. Electrical *pick-up* is eliminated in microphone cables by

    A. keeping the wires straight and without kinks
    B. using shielded wires
    C. holding a hand over the microphone when not talking into it
    D. using solid wires

50. Stranded wires are used in cables rather than solid wires to provide
    A. a smaller cable diameter
    B. greater cable flexibility
    C. reduced electrical interactions between wires
    D. reduced expense in cable manufacture

KEY (CORRECT ANSWERS)

1. D	11. A	21. D	31. C	41. D
2. A	12. D	22. D	32. A	42. A
3. C	13. B	23. A	33. B	43. B
4. A	14. C	24. A	34. A	44. C
5. A	15. A	25. D	35. D	45. B
6. D	16. A	26. A	36. C	46. B
7. B	17. A	27. B	37. A	47. C
8. C	18. B	28. B	38. B	48. A
9. C	19. C	29. A	39. A	49. B
10. B	20. C	30. B	40. A	50. B

TEST 2

DIRECTIONS: Each question or incomplete statement is followed by several suggested answers or completions. Select the one that BEST answers the question or completes the statement. *PRINT THE LETTER OF THE CORRECT ANSWER IN THE SPACE AT THE RIGHT.*

1. A basic element used in producing semiconductor materials is

    A. silicon   B. carbon   C. antimony   D. aluminum

2. The terminals of a diode are called

    A. base and anode
    C. gate and cathode
    B. cathode and anode
    D. emitter and anode

3. With respect to 60-cycle power, one complete cycle takes

    A. 1/60 of a second
    C. 1/60 of a minute
    B. 1/30 of a second
    D. 1/30 of a minute

4. The letters DPDT are used to identify a kind of

    A. fuse   B. cable   C. conduit   D. switch

5. The filament of an incandescent lamp is USUALLY made of

    A. tungsten   B. carbon   C. nickel   D. iron

6. A flashlight battery, a capacitor, and a flashlight bulb are connected in series with each other.
   If the bulb burns brightly and steadily, then the capacitor is

    A. open-circuited
    C. good
    B. short-circuited
    D. fully charged

7. The number of milliamperes in one ampere is

    A. 10   B. 100   C. 1,000   D. 10,000

8. A rectifier changes

    A. D.C. to A.C.
    B. A.C. to D.C.
    C. single-phase to three-phase
    D. battery power to electric power

9. An oscilloscope is an instrument for

    A. measuring noise levels
    B. displaying waveforms of electrical signals
    C. indicating the concentrations of pollutants in air
    D. photographing high speed events

10. A 3-ohm resistor connected directly across a 12-volt battery will draw _____ amperes.

    A. 3   B. 4   C. 12   D. 36

11. If the party on the other end of a radio-telephone line informs you that your voice is distorting, generally it would be BEST for you to

    A. move closer to the microphone
    B. ask the party to raise the volume on his amplifier
    C. speak more softly and move away from the microphone
    D. test your microphone for a possible short circuit

12. According to Fire Department regulations, fire communication radio conversations should be brief and concise, with unnecessary repetition avoided.
    Therefore, lengthy fire communication messages should be transmitted by

    A. telephone   B. telegraph
    C. written report   D. messenger service

13. When receiving a telephone alarm of a fire, the dispatcher needs certain information. Of the following, the MOST important information to be obtained and recorded is the

    A. street address and nearest intersection of the building in which the fire is located
    B. cross streets or avenues near which the telephone is located
    C. location of all persons in the building on fire
    D. name and telephone number of the person making the call

14. Which one of the following statements is the LEAST valid in fire communication?

    A. Radio messages shall be sent at moderate speeds, except when radio fire traffic is heavy.
    B. Personal greetings and pleasantries shall be omitted.
    C. Expressions of courtesy shall be avoided in the interest of brevity.
    D. Indecent and profane language is prohibited.

15. Generally, the preliminary summary of conclusions reached in a report should be placed

    A. near the end of the report
    B. near the beginning of the report
    C. in the middle of the report
    D. between the body of the report and the appendix

16. Of the following, a well-written report generally should NOT

    A. be lengthy
    B. be objective
    C. express documented facts
    D. contain simple vocabulary

Questions 17-21.

  DIRECTIONS: In answering Questions 17 through 21, assume that you are a Fire Alarm Dispatcher.

17. If in the course of an official telephone conversation someone suggests a procedural improvement within your department, of the following, your BEST course of action generally would be to

A. suggest that he write a letter to the Fire Commissioner
B. ask him to elaborate further so that you may write down all the details
C. thank him for the suggestion and tell him that you will bring it to the attention of your supervisor
D. tell him that you have no authority to approve changes, and ask that he call your supervisor directly

18. If you are speaking on the telephone to someone who does not understand a particular word, GENERALLY you should

    A. spell the word and repeat it twice
    B. repeat the word four or five times or until the other person understands
    C. repeat the word in a much louder tone of voice
    D. spell the word and follow each letter with an identifying word beginning with the same letter

19. If you receive a phone call requesting information regarding departmental policy, of the following, your BEST course of action would be to

    A. answer the request as completely as allowable
    B. refer the call to your immediate supervisor
    C. politely tell the caller that departmental policy is not properly the concern of the public
    D. suggest that the caller write a letter to the Fire Commissioner

20. Assume that you have received a telephone call from someone about a fire. The caller is abusive and argumentative.
    Of the following, your BEST course of action would be to

    A. treat him in the same manner as he treats you
    B. immediately transfer the call to another section
    C. reason with the caller in a calm, objective manner
    D. tell him you can not help him until he cools off

21. Over the telephone, you can most effectively convey an attitude of willingness to be of service to the public by

    A. using a friendly, courteous voice
    B. using correct grammar
    C. using a large vocabulary
    D. answering questions in a deliberate and slow manner

22. Fuses are rated in current and

    A. weight   B. voltage   C. wattage   D. hours

23. Continuity of the conductors in a de-energized electrical circuit can be checked by means of a(n)

    A. voltmeter   B. wattmeter
    C. ohmmeter   D. stroboscope

24. If only one-half of a neon tester lights up when placed across two terminals, it should be concluded that

   A. the current across the terminals is A.C.
   B. the current across the terminals is D.C.
   C. one-half of the neon tester is defective
   D. there is an open-circuit at one of the terminals

25. The one of the following substances which is the BEST conductor of electricity is

   A. aluminum   B. copper   C. carbon   D. silver

26. The alphabet used in radio-telephone communications is

   A. Morse   B. Esperanto
   C. phonetic   D. microphonic

27. A type of microphone that employs a diaphragm attached to a coil of wire which is free to move in a magnetic field is a _____ type.

   A. crystal   B. ribbon   C. carbon   D. dynamic

28. Low temperature solder used in electronic work is an alloy consisting of

   A. tin and zinc   B. lead and silver
   C. zinc and lead   D. tin and lead

29. The one of the following which is NOT a part of the alternate system to permit operations of the Bureau of Fire Communications of the Fire Department during a black-out or interruption of power is

   A. power for box alarms independent of the city supply to street lights, etc.
   B. radio power independent of standard local power transmission
   C. an emergency back-up supply provided by local electric utility companies for use by the Fire Department
   D. a back-up battery and a diesel-powered emergency generator for the alarm-sending equipment

30. Code is frequently used in transmitting radio-telephone messages in city departments in order to

   A. speed up the communication process
   B. prevent unauthorized persons from receiving messages
   C. facilitate understanding of messages among department personnel
   D. conform to FCC regulations

Questions 31-40.

DIRECTIONS: Answer Questions 31 through 40 ONLY on the basis of the following information.

Column I consists of serial numbers of dollar bills. Column II shows different ways of arranging the corresponding serial numbers.

5 (#2)

The serial numbers of dollar bills in Column I begin and end with a capital letter and have an eight-digit number in between. The serial numbers in Column I are to be arranged according to the following rules:

First: In alphabetical order according to the first letter.
Second: When two or more serial numbers have the same first letter, in alphabetical order according to the last letter.
Third: When two or more serial numbers have the same first and last letters, in numerical order, beginning with the lowest number.

The serial numbers in Column I are numbered (1) through (5) in the order in which they are listed. In Column II, the numbers (1) through (5) are arranged in four different ways to show different arrangements of the corresponding serial numbers. Choose the answer in Column II in which the serial numbers are arranged according to the above rules.

SAMPLE QUESTION

COLUMN I
1. E75044127B
2. B96399104A
3. B93939086A
4. B47064465H
5. B99040922A

COLUMN II
A. 4, 1, 3, 2, 5
B. 4, 1, 2, 3, 5
C. 4, 3, 2, 5, 1
D. 3, 2, 5, 4, 1

In the sample question, the four serial numbers starting with B should be put before the serial number starting with E. The serial numbers starting with B and ending with A should be put before the serial number starting with B and ending with H. The three serial numbers starting with B and ending with A should be listed in numerical order, beginning with the lowest number. The correct way to arrange the serial numbers, therefore, is:

(3) B93939086A
(2) B96399104A
(5) B99040922A
(4) B47064465H
(1) E75044127B

Since the order of arrangement is 3, 2, 5, 4, 1, the answer to the sample question is D.

COLUMN I

31.
1. D89143888P
2. D98143838B
3. D89113883B
4. D89148338P
5. D89148388B

COLUMN II
A. 3, 5, 2, 1, 4
B. 3, 1, 4, 5, 2
C. 4, 2, 4, 1, 5
D. 4, 1, 3, 5, 2

31.___

6 (#2)

32.	1. W62455599E 2. W62455090F 3. W62405099E 4. V62455097F 5. V62405979E	A. 2, 4, 3, 1, 5 B. 3, 1, 5, 2, 4 C. 5, 3, 1, 4, 2 D. 5, 4, 3, 1, 2				32.____
33.	1. N74663826M 2. M74633286M 3. N76633228N 4. M76483686N 5. M74636688M	A. 2, 4, 5, 3, 1 B. 2, 5, 4, 1, 3 C. 1, 2, 5, 3, 4 D. 2, 5, 1, 4, 3				33.____
34.	1. P97560324B 2. R97663024B 3. P97503024E 4. R97563240E 5. P97652304B	A. 1, 5, 2, 3, 4 B. 3, 1, 4, 5, 2 C. 1, 5, 3, 2, 4 D. 1, 5, 2, 3, 4				34.____
35.	1. H92411165G 2. A92141465G 3. H92141165C 4. H92444165C 5. A92411465G	A. 2, 5, 3, 4, 1 B. 3, 4, 2, 5, 1 C. 3, 2, 1, 5, 4 D. 3, 1, 2, 5, 4				35.____
36.	1. X90637799S 2. N90037696S 3. Y90677369B 4. X09677693B 5. M09673699S	A. 4, 3, 5, 2, 1 B. 5, 4, 2, 1, 3 C. 5, 2, 4, 1, 3 D. 5, 2, 3, 4, 1				36.____
37.	1. K78425174L 2. K78452714C 3. K78547214N 4. K78442774C 5. K78547724M	A. 4, 2, 1, 3, 5 B. 2, 3, 5, 4, 1 C. 1, 4, 2, 3, 5 D. 4, 2, 1, 5, 3				37.____
38.	1. P18736652U 2. P18766352V 3. T17686532U 4. T17865523U 5. P18675332V	A. 1, 3, 4, 5, 2 B. 1, 5, 2, 3, 4 C. 3, 4, 5, 1, 2 D. 5, 2, 1, 3, 4				38.____
39.	1. L51138101K 2. S51138001R 3. S51188111K 4. S51183110R 5. L51188100R	A. 1, 5, 3, 2, 4 B. 1, 3, 5, 2, 4 C. 1, 5, 2, 4, 3 D. 2, 5, 1, 4, 3				39.____

40.
1. J28475446D
2. T28775363D
3. J27843566P
4. T27834563P
5. J28435536D

A. 5, 1, 2, 3, 4
B. 4, 3, 5, 1, 2
C. 1, 5, 2, 4, 3
D. 5, 1, 3, 2, 4

40.___

Questions 41-50.

DIRECTIONS: Answer Questions 41 through 50 ONLY on the basis of the following information.

Each question from 41 through 50 consists of four names. For each question, choose the one of the four names that should be LAST if the four names were arranged in alphabetical order in accordance with the Rules for Alphabetical Filing given below. Read these rules carefully. Then, for each question, indicate in the space at the right the letter before the name that should be LAST in alphabetical order.

RULES FOR ALPHABETICAL FILING

Names of Individuals

1. The names of individuals are filed in strict alphabetical order, first according to last name, then according to first name or initial, and finally according to middle name or initial. For example: George Allen comes before Edward Bell, and Leonard P. Reston comes before Lucille B. Reston.

2. When last names are the same, for example, A. Green and Agnes Green, the one with the initial comes before the one with the name written out when the first initials are identical.

3. When first and last names are alike, the name without a middle initial comes before the one with a middle name or initial. For example: John Doe comes before both John A. Doe and John Alan Doe.

4. When first and last names are the same, the name with a middle initial comes before the one with a middle name beginning with the same initial. For example: Jack R. Hertz comes before Jack Richard Hertz.

5. Prefixes such as De, O', Mac, Mc, and Van are filed as written and are treated as part of the names they come before. For example: Robert O'Dea is filed before David Olsen.

6. Abbreviated names are treated as if they were spelled out. For example: Chas. is filed as Charles and Thos. is filed as Thomas.

7. Titles and designations such as Dr., Mr., and Prof. are disregarded in filing.

Names of Business Organizations

1. The names of business organizations are filed according to the order in which each word in the name appears. When an organization name bears the name of a person, it is filed according to the rules for filing names of people as given above. For example: William Smith Service Co. comes before Television Distributors, Inc.

2. When the following words are part of a business name, they are disregarded: the, of, and.

3. When there are numbers in a name, they are treated as if they were spelled out. For example: 10th Street Bootery is filed as Tenth Street Bootery.

Names of Government Offices

Bureaus, boards, offices, and departments of the city government are filed under the name of the chief governing body. For example: Bureau of the Budget would be filed as if written Budget (Bureau of the).

Sample Question

    A. Jane Earl   (2)
    B. James A. Earle   (4)
    C. James Earl   (1)
    D. J. Earle   (3)

The numbers in parentheses show the proper alphabetical order in which these names should be filed. Since the name that should be filed LAST is James A. Earle, the answer to the Sample Question is B.

41.
    A. Steiner, Michael
    B. Steinblau, Dr. Walter
    C. Steinet, Gary
    D. Stein, Prof. Edward

42.
    A. The Paper Goods Warehouse
    B. T. Pane and Sons Inc.
    C. Paley, Wallace
    D. Painting Supplies Inc.

43.
    A. D'Angelo, F.
    B. De Nove, C.
    C. Daniels, Frank
    D. Dovarre, Carl

44.
    A. Berene, Arnold
    B. Berene, Arnold L.
    C. Beren, Arnold Lee
    D. Berene, A.

45.
    A. Kallinski, Liza
    B. Kalinsky, L.
    C. Kallinky, E.
    D. Kallinsky, Elizabeth

46. A. Morgeno, Salvatore
    B. Megan, J.
    C. J. Morgenthal Consultant Services
    D. Morgan, Janet

46.____

47. A. Ritter, G.
    B. Ritter, George
    C. Riter, George H.
    D. Ritter, G.H.

47.____

48. A. Wheeler, Adele N.
    B. Wieler, Ada
    C. Weiler, Adelaide
    D. Wheiler, Adele

48.____

49. A. Macan, Toby
    B. Maccini, T.
    C. MacAvoy, Thomas
    D. Mackel, Theodore

49.____

50. A. Loomus, Kenneth
    B. Lomis Paper Supplies
    C. Loo, N.
    D. Loomis Machine Repair Company

50.____

KEY (CORRECT ANSWERS)

1. A	11. C	21. A	31. A	41. C
2. B	12. A	22. B	32. D	42. A
3. A	13. A	23. C	33. B	43. D
4. D	14. A	24. B	34. C	44. B
5. A	15. B	25. D	35. A	45. D
6. B	16. A	26. C	36. C	46. C
7. C	17. C	27. D	37. D	47. B
8. B	18. D	28. D	38. B	48. B
9. B	19. A	29. D	39. A	49. D
10. B	20. C	30. A	40. D	50. A

EXAMINATION SECTION
TEST 1

DIRECTIONS: Each question or incomplete statement is followed by several suggested answers or completions. Select the one that BEST answers the question or completes the statement. *PRINT THE LETTER OF THE CORRECT ANSWER IN THE SPACE AT THE RIGHT.*

Questions 1-12.

DIRECTIONS: Questions 1 through 12 are to be answered on the basis of the following information and typical examples.

LIST OF SIGNALS

SIGNAL	MEANING
2-9	Marine Company not required
3	Special building box
4	Battalion Chief
4-4-4	In service signal
4-4-4-4	Return to regular working system
5	Engine Company (Note: Engine companies omit the prelimiary 5 after 4-4-4 preliminary signal, unless used to indicate both sections in service.)
5-7	Engine and ladder company
6	Marine company
6-5	Use telephone
7	Ladder company
8	Squad company
9	Preliminary signal, special units
(a)	Department ambulances (terminals 1, 2, 3, and 4)
(b)	High ladder units (terminals 12 and 13 for 1 and 2, respectively)
(c)	Searchlight units (terminals 21, 22, 23, and 24)
(d)	Mask service unit (terminal 41)
(e)	Thawing apparatus (terminals 51 to 56 for units 1 to 6, respectively)

SIGNAL	MEANING
9-2	Malicious false alarm
10	Rescue company
11	Telegraph test
13(a)	Apparatus unserviceable, when about to proceed to alarm received; or breaks down during response to alarm
(b)	Apparatus unserviceable, while in quarters or in field during inspectional activities, etc., prior to receipt of alarm
(c)	Engine or ladder company stops to extinguish fire while responding to another alarm; or while returning from an alarm and additional help required (Note: Engine company to use preliminary 5)
14	Increase, reduce, or shutdown pressure on high pressure system
15	Relocation of engine company
16	Relocation of marine company
17	Relocation of ladder company

2 (#1)

The following examples illustrate the use of the signals shown on pages 1 and 2.

SIGNAL	EXAMPLES EXPLANATION
4-4-4--5--21 (Note A.)	Both sections of Engine Co. 21 in service (Signal 4-4-4 is the preliminary indicating <u>in service</u>. Here it is followed by the unit preliminary 5 designating both sections of an engine company and the unit number.)
4-4-4--53--46 (Note B.)	Engine Co. 53 in service; Engine Co. 46 relocated (When a company relocates, the in service signal 4-4-4 is transmitted for the company which is in service and the number of the company that relocates is added. Engine companies omit the preliminary 5.)

SIGNAL	EXPLANATION
4-4-4--7--33--11	Ladder Co. 33 is in service; Ladder Co. 11 relocated. (See Note B above.) Here the preliminary 7 indicating ladder company cannot be omitted.)
5-831-21 (Note C.)	Special call for Engine Co. 21 to box 831. (Signal 5 is the preliminary for an engine company. It is followed by the box number, then by the company number.)
6-33-2	Special call for Marine Company 2 to box 33. (For sequence, see explanation in Note C above.) (Signal 6 is the preliminary for a Marine company.)
6--2--6-5 (Note D).	Marine Company 2 to call dispatcher on the telephone. (Signal 6-5 directs the receiver to call the dispatcher on the telephone. In this case, the receiver is Marine Company 2, whose unit preliminary and unit number precedes the signal 6-5.)
7-831-23	Special call for Ladder Company 23 to box 831. (Signal 7 is the preliminary for a ladder company. For sequence, see explanation Note C above.)
9-831-2 (Note E.)	Special call for Department Ambulance #2 to box 831. (Signal 9 is the preliminary for specially equipped units. As indicated in 9(a) in the list of signals, 2 is the designation for Dept. Ambulance #2. The sequence follows explanation in Note C above.)

3 (#1)

4-4-4--9--52 (Note F.)	Indicates Thawing Unit 2 in service (Signal 4-4-4 is preliminary for in service; 9 is preliminary for special unit; 52 designates Thawing Unit #2 as indicated in 9(e) in the list of signals. For meanings of other terminals see list of signals 9(a), (b), (c), (d).
13-2	Unserviceability of Engine Co. 2

SIGNAL	EXPLANATION
(Note G.)	(Preliminary 13 has three related meanings as indicated in the list of signals. Here it indicates unserviceability. It is followed by 2 to indicate Engine Company 2; preliminary 5 is omitted in this case.)
13-7-1 (Note H.)	Ladder Co. 1 out of service (Explanation same as in Note G except that the preliminary 7, indicating a ladder company, cannot be omitted.)
13-5-620-2 (Note I.)	Engine Co. 2 has stopped to extinguish a fire near box 620. (Signal 13 is also used as a preliminary to indicate that a company has stopped to extinguish a fire while responding to another location. The sequence of signals is: preliminary 13, unit preliminary (engine companies use preliminary 5), street box number nearest fire, number of the company.)
15-40-34 (Note J.)	Special call for Engine Co. 34 to relocate in quarters of Engine Co. 40. (An engine company may be relocated in the quarters of another company by use of the following signal: preliminary 15, number of company to be covered, number of company which shall relocate.)
16-2-4 (Note K.)	Special call for Marine Company 4 to relocate at berth of Marine Company 2. (Signal 16 is a preliminary for marine company to change location. See note J above for sequence.)
17-3-4 (Note L.)	Special call for Ladder Co. 4 to relocate in the quarters of Ladder Co. 3 (Signal 17 is a preliminary for ladder company to change location. See note J above for sequence.)

1. The signal 4-4-4--9--24 means

    A. Engine Co. 24 is in service
    B. Engine Co. 24 in service; Engine Co. 9 relocated
    C. Searchlight Unit #24 in service
    D. Engine Companies 9 and 24 in service

2. The signal 4-4-4--4--9 means

    A. regular working tours for Engine Co. 9
    B. Engine Co. 9 in service; Engine Co. 4 relocated
    C. Department Ambulance 4 in service
    D. 9th Battalion in service

3. The signal on which Searchlight Unit 23 would respond to box 432 is

    A. 432-9-23   B. 9-432-23   C. 23-432-9   D. 9-23-432

4. The signal 9-273-41
    A. indicates Mask Service Unit out of service
    B. is a special call for Mask Service Unit to box 273
    C. indicates Mask Service Unit is not required
    D. is a special call for Marine Company 41 to box 273

5. The signal 17-38-32 indicates
    A. a special call for Engine Co. 32 to relocate in quarters of Engine Co. 38
    B. a special call for Engine Co. 32 to box 38
    C. a special call for Ladder Co. 32 to relocate in the quarters of Ladder Co. 38
    D. Ladder Co. 38 to relocate in the quarters of Ladder Co. 32

6. The meaning of signal 9-2--831 is
    A. special call for Department Ambulance 2 to box 831
    B. marine company not required at box 831
    C. special call for Thawing Apparatus 2 to box 831
    D. malicious false alarm at box 831

7. The signal 13-7-5 indicates
    A. unserviceability of Engine Co. 5
    B. unserviceability of Ladder Co. 5
    C. Engine Co. 7 has stopped at box 5 to extinguish a fire
    D. Ladder Co. 5 has stopped at box 7 to extinguish a fire

8. The signal 13-7-319-5 means
    A. Ladder Co. 5 has stopped to extinguish a fire near box 619
    B. Engine Co. 7 has stopped to extinguish a fire near box 619
    C. Ladder Co. 5 out of service
    D. Engine Co. 7 out of service

9. The signal which is a special call for Engine Co. 24 to box 721 is
    A. 5-721-24   B. 7-721-24   C. 721-24-5   D. 24-721-7

10. The special call for Marine Co. 5 to relocate at berth of Marine Co. 3 is
    A. 16-5-3   B. 6-3-5   C. 16-3-5   D. 3-16-5

11. The signal 4-4-4--9--13 means
    A. Engine Co. 13 in service; Engine Co. 9 relocated
    B. High Ladder Unit 2 in service
    C. Engine Companies 9 and 13 in service
    D. Engine Co. 13 in service

12. The signal 7--17--6-5 means Ladder Co(s).
    A. 5 to relocate in quarters of Ladder Co. 6
    B. 5 and 6 to go to box 17
    C. 17 to call dispatcher on the telephone
    D. 5 to relocate in quarters of Ladder Co. 6

KEY (CORRECT ANSWERS)

1. C
2. D
3. B
4. B
5. C
6. D
7. B
8. A
9. A
10. C
11. B
12. C

TEST 2

DIRECTIONS: Each question or incomplete statement is followed by several suggested answers or completions. Select the one that BEST answers the question or completes the statement. *PRINT THE LETTER OF THE CORRECT ANSWER IN THE SPACE AT THE RIGHT.*

Questions 1-7.

DIRECTIONS: Questions 1 through 7 are to be answered on the basis of the following information.

TRANSMISSION INSTRUCTIONS

A cipher (0) is represented by 10 consecutive taps.

All numerals above 9 (except 11 to represent company, battalion or division number or termination of company number; and signals 10, 11, 12, 13, 14, 15, 16, 17, and 18) are made up of taps and spaces. The exceptions are made up of consecutive taps.

There is a pause (equivalent to about 3 spaces) between signals.

EXAMPLE 1: Box 10: 1 tap, space, 10 consecutive taps
EXAMPLE 2: Engine Co. 211: 2 taps, space, 11 consecutive taps
EXAMPLE 3: Preliminary 13: 13 consecutive taps
EXAMPLE 4: 5-131-4 (Engine Co. 4 to box 131): 5 taps, pause, 1 tap, space, 3 taps, space, 1 tap, pause, 4 taps

1. In accordance with the above information, assume that the number of a certain box is transmitted as follows: 1 tap, space, 10 consecutive taps, space, 1 tap, space, 10 consecutive taps.
   The number of this box is

   A. 110110   B. 10110   C. 1010   D. 11010

2. In accordance with the information given above, the one of the following which shows the proper transmission of signal 7-831-6 (Ladder Co. 6 to box 831) is

   A. 7 taps, space, 8 taps, space, 3 taps, space, 1 tap, space, 6 taps
   B. 7 taps, pause, 8 taps, space, 3 taps, space, 1 tap, pause, 6 taps
   C. 7 taps, pause, 8 taps, space, 3 taps, space, 1 tap, space, 6 taps
   D. 7 taps, pause, 8 taps, pause, 3 taps, pause, 1 tap, space, 6 taps

3. In accordance with the information given above, the one of the following which shows the proper transmission of signal 10-723-2 (Rescue Co. 2 to Box 723) is

   A. 10 consecutive taps, pause, 7 taps, space, 2 taps, space, 3 taps, pause, 2 taps
   B. 1 tap, space, 10 taps, pause, 7 taps, space, 2 taps, space, 3 taps, pause, 2 taps
   C. 1 tap, space, 10 taps, space, 7 taps, space, 2 taps, space, 3 taps, pause, 2 taps
   D. 10 consecutive taps, pause, 7 taps, space, 2 taps, space, 3 taps, space, 2 taps

1.___

2.___

3.___

4. In accordance with the information given above, the one of the following which shows the proper transmission of signal 13-7-21 (unserviceability of Ladder Co. 21) is

   A. 13 consecutive taps, pause, 7 taps, space, 2 taps, space, 1 tap
   B. 1 tap, space, 3 taps, pause, 7 taps, pause, 2 taps, space, 1 tap
   C. 1 tap, space, 3 taps, pause, 7 taps, space, 2 taps, space, 1 tap
   D. 13 consecutive taps, pause, 7 taps, pause, 2 taps, space, 1 tap

4.____

5. In accordance with the information given above, the one of the following which shows the proper transmission of the signal 9-810-3 (special call for Department Ambulance 3 to box 810) is

   A. 9 taps, pause, 8 taps, space, 10 consecutive taps, space, 3 taps
   B. 9 taps, space, 8 taps, space, 1 tap, space, 10 taps, space, 3 taps
   C. 9 taps, pause, 8 taps, space, 1 tap, space, 10 consecutive taps, pause, 3 taps
   D. 9 taps, space, 8 taps, space, 10 consecutive taps, pause, 3 taps

5.____

6. In accordance with the information given above, the one of the following which shows the proper transmission of the signal 7-411-211 (Ladder Co. 211 to box 411) is

   A. 7 taps, pause, 4 taps, space, 1 tap, space, 1 tap, pause, 2 taps, space, 1 tap, space, 1 tap
   B. 7 taps, pause, 4 taps, space, 1 tap, space, 1 tap, pause, 2 taps, space, 11 consecutive taps
   C. 7 taps, pause, 4 taps, space, 11 consecutive taps, pause, 2 taps, space, 1 tap, space, 1 tap
   D. 7 taps, pause, 4 taps, space, 11 consecutive taps, pause, 2 taps, space, 11 consecutive taps

6.____

7. In accordance with the information given in the Transmission Instructions on the previous page, the one of the following which shows the proper transmission of the signal 15-111-311 (special call for Engine Co. 311 to relocate in the quarters of Engine Co. 111) is

   A. 1 tap, space, 5 taps, pause, 1 tap, space, 11 consecu-ive taps, pause, 3 taps, space, 11 consecutive taps
   B. 15 consecutive taps, pause, 11 consecutive taps, space, 1 tap, pause, 3 taps, space, 11 consecutive taps
   C. 15 consecutive taps, pause, 1 tap, space, 11 consecutive taps, pause, 3 taps, space, 11 consecutive taps
   D. 1 tap, space, 5 taps, pause, 1 tap, space, 1 tap, space, 1 tap, pause, 3 taps, space, 1 tap, space, 1 tap

7.____

KEY (CORRECT ANSWERS)

1. C
2. B
3. A
4. D
5. C
6. B
7. C

TEST 3

DIRECTIONS: Each question or incomplete statement is followed by several suggested answers or completions. Select the one that BEST answers the question or completes the statement. *PRINT THE LETTER OF THE CORRECT ANSWER IN THE SPACE AT THE RIGHT.*

1. The resistance of a piece of copper wire is

    A. *inversely* proportional to its length
    B. *directly* proportional to its diameter
    C. *inversely* proportional to its cross-sectional area
    D. *directly* proportional to the square of its diameter

    1.___

2. Of the following, the instrument BEST suited to test the charge of a battery is the

    A. bolometer   B. barometer
    C. hygrometer   D. hydrometer

    2.___

3. Assume that a relay coil having a resistance of 22 ohms is connected across a supply of 110 volts D.C.
   The current, in amperes, in the coil is MOST NEARLY

    A. 0.2   B. 0.5   C. 4.4   D. 5

    3.___

4. If a fuse of higher rating than the current rating of the circuit is used in an electrical circuit,

    A. maintenance of the larger fuse will be higher
    B. better protection will be obtained
    C. serious damage may result to the circuit from overload
    D. the fuse will blow more often since it carries more current

    4.___

5. Assume that resistances of 2, 4, and 5 ohms, respectively, are connected in series.
   The resistance of this combination, in ohms, is MOST NEARLY

    A. .95   B. 1.05   C. 11   D. 45

    5.___

6. Assume that three 2-ohm resistances are connected in parallel.
   The resistance of this combination, in ohms, is MOST NEARLY

    A. .66   B. 1.5   C. 6   D. 8

    6.___

7. Defects in wiring which cause current to flow from one wire to another before the intended path has been completed are called

    A. opens   B. shorts
    C. electrolysis   D. breaks

    7.___

8. A coil having 60 turns of #12 wire as compared to a coil of the same diameter but having only 30 turns of #12 wire has

    A. the same impedance   B. the same inductance
    C. a larger inductance   D. a smaller inductance

    8.___

9. Assume that a condenser having a capacitance of one microfarad is connected in parallel with a condenser having a capacitance of 2 microfarads.
The combination is equal to a condenser having a capacitance, in microfarads, of MOST NEARLY

   A. .66   B. 1.5   C. 2   D. 3

10. The one of the following substances which is the BEST conductor of electricity is

    A. iron   B. aluminum   C. copper   D. tin

11. The number of milliamperes which is equivalent to one ampere is

    A. 10,000   B. 1,000   C. 100   D. 10

12. The symbol, ⏚ often shown in a wiring diagram, indicates a

    A. ground
    B. resistor
    C. capacitor
    D. lightning arrester

13. The electromotive force that is MOST likely induced in a loop of wire rotating between the poles of a permanent magnet is

    A. AC
    B. rectified AC
    C. pulsating DC
    D. DC

14. Assume that a condenser having a capacitance of 2 micro-farads is connected in series with a condenser having a capacitance of 3 microfarads.
The combination will be equal to a condenser having a capacitance, in microfarads, of MOST NEARLY

    A. .83   B. 1.2   C. 5   D. 6

15. To measure the speed of the shaft of a generator directly in rpm, it is BEST to use a

    A. psychrometer
    B. chronometer
    C. manometer
    D. tachometer

16. The one of the following readings of the specific gravity of the electrolyte of a lead acid storage battery which indicates a completely discharged battery is

    A. 1.610   B. 1.260   C. 1.160   D. 1.260

17. The one of the following readings of the specific gravity of the electrolyte of a lead acid storage battery which MOST NEARLY indicates a charged battery is

    A. 1.610   B. 1.260   C. 1.160   D. 1.020

18. Assume that the level of the electrolyte in a fully charged lead acid storage battery has fallen due to evaporation.
The one of the following substances which it is BEST to add in order to restore the electrolyte to its original level is

    A. sulphate spring water
    B. potassium hydroxide
    C. distilled water
    D. sulphuric acid

19. The PROPER way to reverse the direction of rotation of a 3-phase wound rotor induction motor is to

    A. shift the brushes
    B. reverse two leads between the rotor and the control resistance
    C. open one rotor lead
    D. reverse two supply leads

20. The direction of rotation of a DC shunt motor can be reversed properly by

    A. shifting the position of the brushes
    B. reversing the connections to the field
    C. reversing two supply leads
    D. reversing the connections to both the armature and the field

21. A direct current supply may be obtained from an alternating current source by the use of which one of the following?
    A(n)

    A. inductance-capacitance filter
    B. frequency changer set
    C. tungar bulb
    D. inverter

22. The one of the following which is the MOST common type of motor that can be used with either an AC or a DC source is the _____ motor.

    A. shunt
    B. induction
    C. repulsion
    D. series

23. A piece of fine emery cloth should be used to smooth down the commutator of a DC generator

    A. when the commutator is rough or worn
    B. whenever there is sparking at the brushes
    C. when the brushes do not make good contact
    D. under no circumstances

24. Assume that a positively non-interfering and succession type of fire alarm box is operated while another similar box is in operation on the same circuit. Under these circumstances,

    A. there will be overlapping of signals so that the location of the fire cannot be accurately determined
    B. the signal from the second box will be partly or completely suppressed until the signal from the first box has been received
    C. none of the signals will be lost or interfered with, but will be delayed and transmitted in order of box operation
    D. the box nearest the fire will take over

25. The one of the following items which is commonly used to increase the range of a DC ammeter is a(n)

    A. current transformer
    B. bridging transformer
    C. shunt
    D. inverter

26. The one of the following which should be used to test whether a circuit is AC or DC is a

   A. hot wire ammeter
   B. neon light
   C. pair of test lamps
   D. bolometer

27. The term *open circuit* means that the

   A. circuit has one end exposed
   B. wiring is exposed
   C. circuit is not continuous
   D. service switch is located outdoors

28. Continuity of the conductors in an electrical circuit can be determined conveniently by means of a(n)

   A. bell and battery set
   B. magnet
   C. Preece test
   D. anemometer

29. Assume that an alternator driven by a diesel engine supplies AC current at a frequency of 50 cycles per second.
    In order to change the frequency to 60 cycles per second, it is necessary to

   A. *increase* the field strength
   B. *decrease* the field strength
   C. *increase* the speed of the diesel engine
   D. *decrease* the speed of the diesel engine

30. A starting device which will limit the starting current of a DC motor is generally required because

   A. an increased starting torque is obtained by decreasing the starting current
   B. the counter e.m.f. is zero at standstill
   C. the inertia of the driven load causes excessive starting current
   D. the counter e.m.f. is maximum at standstill

31. Standard radio and audio frequencies are broadcast continuously from _____ operated by the _____.

   A. WWV; central radio propagation laboratory
   B. WNYC; Bureau of Standards and Appeals
   C. WNJC; Bureau of Standards and Appeals
   D. WNYE; F.C.C.

32. The one of the following which is used in some communications receivers to indicate the strength of the received signal in arbitrary units is a(n) _____ meter.

   A. S
   B. VU
   C. decibel
   D. Q

33. Assume that you are tuning the tank circuit of a crystal oscillator and simultaneously note the reading of the grid milliameter in the following stage.
    When the tuning is correct, this milliameter should indicate _____ value.

   A. a maximum
   B. a minimum
   C. zero
   D. a rapidly fluctuating

34. The term VU refers to

   A. volume expansion
   B. the audio-frequency power level in decibels above a reference level of 1 milliwatt
   C. the audio-frequency power level in decibels above a reference level of 6 milliwatts
   D. unmodulated peak voltage

35. An oscillator in which an audio frequency is obtained by mixing together two radio frequencies is known as a

   A. master oscillator
   B. crystal oscillator
   C. limiter
   D. beat frequency oscillator

36. In a high level A.M. transmitter, modulation takes place in the

   A. buffer amplifier
   B. intermediate power amplifier
   C. output amplifier
   D. oscillator

37. For proper operation, before transmitting, radio units require

   A. a dummy antenna
   B. the insertion of an isolating transformer
   C. a warm-up time
   D. checking for proper multiplexing

38. Water should NOT be used to extinguish fires in or around electrical apparatus. The MAIN reason for this is that water

   A. may conduct electric current and cause a shock hazard
   B. may cause the circuit fuses to blow
   C. will corrode the electrical conductors
   D. will damage insulation

39. One should be extremely careful to keep open flames and sparks away from batteries when they are being charged because the

   A. sulphate given off during this operation is highly flammable
   B. hydrogen given off during this operation is highly flammable
   C. static electricity of the battery may cause combustion
   D. oxygen given off during this operation is highly flammable

40. Artificial respiration should be started immediately on a man who has suffered electric shock if he is

   A. unconscious and breathing
   B. conscious and badly burned
   C. in a daze, although conscious
   D. unconscious and not breathing

Questions 41-43.

DIRECTIONS: Questions 41 through 43 are to be answered on the basis of the following statement.

The manual of Fire Communications was planned to serve the Fire Department as guide and reference in effective use of its vast, versatile communications network.... Complete understanding of its phases and precepts, together with prompt compliance with all requirements and actions set in motion by its coded signals and radio transmissions, are essential.

41. The word *versatile,* as used in the above statement, means MOST NEARLY 41.____

    A. steady B. many-sided
    C. constant D. wavering

42. The word *precepts,* as used in the above statement, means MOST NEARLY 42.____

    A. forerunners B. paragraphs
    C. rules D. sections

43. The word *compliance,* as used in the above statement, means MOST NEARLY 43.____

    A. variance B. dissension
    C. divergence D. conformance

44. Any major components of a Fire Communication system should be meticulously maintained. In the preceding sentence, the word *meticulously* means MOST NEARLY 44.____

    A. indifferently B. perfunctorily
    C. painstakingly D. languidly

Questions 45-47.

DIRECTIONS: Questions 45 through 47 are to be answered in accordance with the following statements.
In order to facilitate prompt assembly of designated members, the officer in charge, Bureau of Fire Communications, shall maintain accurate current data on all such matters.

45. The word *facilitate,* as used in the above statement, means MOST NEARLY 45.____

    A. authorize B. expedite C. command D. hinder

46. The word *designated,* as used in the above statement, means MOST NEARLY 46.____

    A. required B. versatile C. skillful D. selected

47. The word *data,* as used in the above statement, means MOST NEARLY 47.____

    A. calculations B. information
    C. forecasts D. surveillance

Questions 48-49.

DIRECTIONS: Questions 48 and 49 are to be answered in accordance with the following statement.

In the event of severe <u>disruption</u> of circuits...members of this squad may be...<u>detailed</u> to Bureau of Fire Communications for duration of such emergency.

48. The word *disruption,* as used in the above sentence, means MOST NEARLY 48.___

    A. overloading   B. breakdown
    C. disuse   D. concurrence

49. The word *detailed,* as used in the above statement, means MOST NEARLY 49.___

    A. assigned   B. reported   C. demoted   D. promoted

50. The officer in command, after <u>verification</u> that the alarm was false, shall transmit by radio the signal 9-2 followed by box number. 50.___
The word *verification,* as used in the preceding sentence, means MOST NEARLY

    A. confirmation   B. consideration
    C. notification   D. confutation

KEY (CORRECT ANSWERS)

1. C	11. B	21. C	31. A	41. B
2. D	12. A	22. D	32. A	42. C
3. D	13. A	23. D	33. A	43. D
4. C	14. B	24. C	34. B	44. C
5. C	15. D	25. C	35. D	45. B
6. A	16. C	26. B	36. C	46. D
7. B	17. B	27. C	37. C	47. B
8. C	18. C	28. A	38. A	48. B
9. D	19. D	29. C	39. B	49. A
10. C	20. B	30. B	40. D	50. A

EXAMINATION SECTION
TEST 1

DIRECTIONS: Each question or incomplete statement is followed by several suggested answers or completions. Select the one that BEST answers the question or completes the statement. *PRINT THE LETTER OF THE CORRECT ANSWER IN THE SPACE AT THE RIGHT.*

1. The transmission of signals by electromagnetic waves is referred to as

    A. biotelemetry
    B. radio
    C. noise
    D. all of the above

    1.____

2. The transmission of physiologic data, such as an ECG, from the patient to a distant point of reception is called

    A. biotelemetry
    B. simplex
    C. landline
    D. none of the above

    2.____

3. The assembly of a transmitter, receiver, and antenna connection at a fixed location creates a

    A. transceiver
    B. radio
    C. biotelemetry
    D. base station

    3.____

4. The portion of the radio frequency spectrum between 30 and 150 mhz is called

    A. very high frequency (VHF)
    B. ultrahigh frequency (UHF)
    C. very low frequency (VLF)
    D. all of the above

    4.____

5. A _____ is a miniature transmitter that picks up a radio signal and rebroadcasts it, thus extending the range of a radiocommunication system.

    A. transceiver   B. repeater   C. simplex   D. duplex

    5.____

6. The portion of the radio frequency spectrum falling between 300 and 3,000 mhz is called

    A. ultrahigh frequency (UHF)
    B. very high frequency (VHF)
    C. very low frequency (VLF)
    D. none of the above

    6.____

7. One cycle per second equals one _____ in units of frequency.

    A. hertz   B. kilohertz   C. megahertz   D. gigahertz

    7.____

8. The sources of noise in ECG telemetry include

    A. loose ECG electrodes
    B. muscle tremors
    C. sources of 60-cycle alternating current such as transformers, power lines, and electric equipment
    D. all of the above

    8.____

9. The method of radio communications called _____ utilizes a single frequency that enables either transmission or reception of either voice or an ECG signal, but is incapable of simultaneous transmission and reception.

    A. duplex
    B. simplex
    C. multiplex
    D. none of the above

10. A terminal that receives transmissions of telemetry and voice from the field and transmits messages back through the base is referred to as a

    A. transceiver
    B. remote control
    C. remote console
    D. ten-code

11. The role of dispatcher includes

    A. reception of requests for help
    B. arrangements for getting the appropriate people and equipment to a situation which requires them
    C. deciding upon and dispatching of the appropriate emergency vehicles
    D. all of the above

12. A dispatcher should NOT

    A. maintain records
    B. scope a problem by requesting additional information from a caller
    C. direct public safety personnel
    D. receive notification of emergencies and call for assistance from both individual citizens and public safety units

13. The professional society of public safety communicators has developed a standard set of ten codes, the MOST common of which is 10-

    A. 1
    B. 4
    C. 12
    D. 18

14. What is the meaning of 10-33?

    A. Help me quick
    B. Arrived at scene
    C. Reply to message
    D. Disregard

15. One of the MAIN purposes of ten-codes is to

    A. shorten air time
    B. complicate the message
    C. increase the likelihood of misunderstanding
    D. none of the above

Questions 16-20.

DIRECTIONS: In Questions 16 through 20, match each translation of a commonly used ten-code with its appropriate code, listed in Column I.

COLUMN I

A. 10-1
B. 10-9
C. 10-18
D. 10-20
E. 10-23

16. What is your location? 16.____

17. Urgent. 17.____

18. Signal weak. 18.____

19. Arrived at the scene. 19.____

20. Please repeat. 20.____

KEY (CORRECT ANSWERS)

1.	B	11.	D
2.	A	12.	C
3.	D	13.	B
4.	A	14.	A
5.	B	15.	A
6.	D	16.	D
7.	A	17.	C
8.	D	18.	A
9.	B	19.	E
10.	C	20.	B

TEST 2

DIRECTIONS: Each question or incomplete statement is followed by several suggested answers or completions. Select the one that BEST answers the question or completes the statement. *PRINT THE LETTER OF THE CORRECT ANSWER IN THE SPACE AT THE RIGHT.*

1. FCC rules prohibit

    A. deceptive or unnecessary messages
    B. profanity
    C. dissemination or use of confidential information transmitted over the radio
    D. all of the above

    1.____

2. Penalties for violations of FCC rules and regulations range from

    A. prison to death
    B. $20,000 to $100,000
    C. $100 to $10,000 and up to one year in prison
    D. up to 10 years in prison

    2.____

3. Which of the following is NOT true about base stations?

    A. The terrain and location do not affect the function.
    B. A good high-gain antenna improves transmission and reception efficiency.
    C. Multiple frequency capability is available at the base station.
    D. Antenna should be as close as possible to the base station transmitter/receiver.

    3.____

4. Radio frequencies are designated by cycles per second. 1,000,000 cycles per second equals one

    A. kilohertz   B. megahertz   C. gigahertz   D. hertz

    4.____

5. The Federal Communications Commission (FCC) is the agency of the United States government responsible for

    A. licensing and frequency allocation
    B. establishing technical standards for radio equipment
    C. establishing and enforcing rules and regulations for the operation of radio equipment
    D. all of the above

    5.____

6. Information relayed to the physician should include all of the following EXCEPT

    A. patient's age, sex, and chief complaint
    B. pertinent history of present illness
    C. detailed family history
    D. pertinent physical findings

    6.____

7. True statements regarding UHF band may include all of the following EXCEPT:

   A. It has better penetration in the dense metropolitan area
   B. Reception is usually quiet inside the building
   C. It has a longer range than VHF band
   D. Most medical communications occur around 450 to 470 mhz

8. Which of the following statements is NOT true regarding VHF band?

   A. Low band frequency may have ranges up to 2000 miles, but are unpredictable.
   B. VHF band may cause *skip interference,* with patchy losses in communication.
   C. High band frequency is wholly free of skip interference.
   D. High band frequencies for emergency medical purposes are in the 300 to 3000 mhz range.

9. 1000 cycles per second is equal to one

   A. hertz   B. kilohertz   C. megahertz   D. gigahertz

10. _____ achieves simultaneous transmission of voice and ECG signals over a single radio frequency.

    A. Duplex
    B. Multiplex
    C. Channel
    D. None of the above

11. Radio equipment used for both VHF and UHF band is

    A. frequency modulated
    B. amplitude modulated
    C. double amplitude modulated
    D. all of the above

12. ECG telemetry over UHF frequencies is confined to _____ of a 12 lead ECG.

    A. 1   B. 2   C. 6   D. 12

13. All of the following further clarity and conciseness EXCEPT

    A. understandable rate of speaking
    B. knowing what you want to transmit after transmission
    C. clear presentation of numbers, names, and dates
    D. using phrases and words which are easy to copy

14. The LEAST preferred of the following words is

    A. check   B. desire   C. want   D. advise if

15. All of the following are techniques useful during a call EXCEPT

    A. answering promptly
    B. identifying yourself and your department
    C. speaking directly into the mouthpiece
    D. none of the above

Questions 16-20.

DIRECTIONS: In Questions 16 through 20, match each definition with the term it describes, listed in Column I.

COLUMN I
A. Frequency
B. Noise
C. Patch
D. Duplex
E. Transceiver

16. A radio transmitter and receiver housed in a single unit; a two-way radio

17. The number of cycles per second of a radio signal, inversely related to the wavelength.

18. Interference in radio signals.

19. A radio system employing more than one frequency to permit simultaneous transmission and reception.

20. Connection between a telephone line and a radio communication system, enabling a caller to get *on the air* by special telephone.

KEY (CORRECT ANSWERS)

1.	D	11.	A
2.	C	12.	A
3.	A	13.	B
4.	B	14.	C
5.	D	15.	D
6.	C	16.	E
7.	C	17.	A
8.	D	18.	B
9.	B	19.	D
10.	B	20.	C

EXAMINATION SECTION
TEST 1

DIRECTIONS: Each question or incomplete statement is followed by several suggested answers or completions. Select the one that BEST answers the question or completes the statement. *PRINT THE LETTER OF THE CORRECT ANSWER IN THE SPACE AT THE RIGHT.*

1. The term for the place at which the control operator function is performed is the   1.____

    A. operating desk
    B. control point
    C. station
    D. manual control location

2. Before transmitting on any frequency, an operator should   2.____

    A. listen to make sure your signal will be heard
    B. make sure the standing-wave ratio on the antenna feed line is high enough
    C. listen to make sure others are not using the frequency
    D. check the antenna for resonance at the selected frequency

3. The _____ sideband is COMMONLY used for 10-meter phone operation.   3.____

    A. lower
    B. upper
    C. amplitude-compandored
    D. double

4. Which type of system does NOT permit the transmission and reception of any signals to take place at the same time?   4.____

    A. Repeater   B. Simplex   C. Remote   D. Duplex

5. Radio emissions are considered *wideband* if their deviation amounts are greater than a MINIMUM of _____ kHz.   5.____

    A. 10   B. 1   C. 15   D. 5

6. When a signal report is referred to as *three three*,   6.____

    A. its contact is serial number thirty-three
    B. it is unreadable and very weak
    C. it is readable with considerable difficulty
    D. its station is located at thirty-three degrees latitude

7. Generally, the type of communications that are capable of the GREATEST range are _____ band.   7.____

    A. low   B. high   C. aviation   D. side

8. For two-way systems situated in and around an urban area, what block of frequencies are allocated for use by mobile telephone services operated by common carriers? _____ MHz.   8.____

    A. 30   B. 40   C. 470-512   D. 900

9. The basic unit of electrical power is the   9.____

    A. ohm   B. ampere   C. volt   D. watt

10. In the radio transmission of speech, the amplification used at the receiver to maintain the natural balance of high and low speech frequencies is referred to as

    A. preemphasis
    B. deemphasis
    C. loading
    D. squelch

11. An antenna that is mounted horizontally would be MOST suitable for the reception of _____ polarized _____.

    A. horizontally; voltages
    B. vertically; waves
    C. vertically; voltages
    D. horizontally; waves

12. What is the PROPER distress call to use when operating a radiotelephone?

    A. MAYDAY   B. HELP   C. EMERGENCY   D. SOS

13. A two-way FM transmitter should be adjusted for a deviation that will produce a bandwidth _____ AM transmitter.

    A. less than that produced by an equivalently modulated
    B. greater than that produced by an equivalently modulated
    C. equal to that produced by an equivalently modulated
    D. that will not be capable of interacting with an

14. The term for the transmission of signals OUTSIDE the intended band is

    A. spurious emissions
    B. off-frequency emissions
    C. side tones
    D. chirping

15. Which of the following is TRUE of FM radio systems?

    A. The frequency is constant and the amplitude is varied.
    B. The amplitude is constant and the frequency is varied.
    C. The frequency and the amplitude are varied.
    D. Neither the frequency nor the amplitude is modulated.

16. During daytime hours, the BEST band for communications over a distance of 200 miles is the _____-m band.

    A. 160   B. 80   C. 40   D. 6

17. A transmission that disturbs other communications is called

    A. transponder signals
    B. unidentified transmissions
    C. harmful interference
    D. interrupted CW

18. A buzzing or hum in the signal of a high-frequency transmitter is USUALLY caused by

    A. an antenna of the wrong length
    B. a bad filter capacitor in the power supply
    C. energy from another transmitter
    D. a badly-designed power output circuit

19. If an operator's signal is extremely strong and perfectly readable, what adjustment should be made to the transmitter?

    A. Turn on the speech processor
    B. Turn down the power output
    C. Reduce the frequency
    D. Reduce the standing-wave ratio

    19._____

20. What is generally considered to be the reliable range for UHF communications? _____ km.

    A. 20   B. 40   C. 60   D. 80

    20._____

21. If a transmitter is operated WITHOUT the cover in place, it may

    A. transmit a weak signal
    B. transmit a chirping signal
    C. transmit onto unintended bands
    D. interfere with other transmitters operating on the same frequency

    21._____

22. In transmitters used to convey speech, the deviation for the given amplitude

    A. increases as the modulation signal increases
    B. decreases as the modulation signal increases
    C. remains roughly half of the modulation signal
    D. is the same regardless of the frequency of the modulation signal

    22._____

23. The purpose of a limiter in an FM receiver is to limit the

    A. audio output
    B. amplitude of the intermediate frequency signal fed to the detector
    C. gain of the radio frequency amplifier
    D. amplitude of the detected output signal

    23._____

24. The FASTEST code speed a repeater may use for automatic identification is _____ words per minute.

    A. 10   B. 20
    C. 40   D. no limit

    24._____

25. The purpose of a squelch control is to

    A. set the sensitivity of the squelch circuit
    B. squelch all undesired noise signals
    C. set the limit of the noise amplitude
    D. squelch interference signals

    25._____

KEY (CORRECT ANSWERS)

1. B
2. C
3. B
4. B
5. D

6. C
7. A
8. B
9. D
10. B

11. D
12. A
13. C
14. A
15. B

16. C
17. C
18. B
19. B
20. B

21. C
22. D
23. B
24. B
25. A

TEST 2

DIRECTIONS: Each question or incomplete statement is followed by several suggested answers or completions. Select the one that BEST answers the question or completes the statement. *PRINT THE LETTER OF THE CORRECT ANSWER IN THE SPACE AT THE RIGHT.*

1. The basic unit of electrical resistance is the   1._____

   A. watt   B. ampere   C. volt   D. ohm

2. An autopatch is a device that   2._____

   A. automatically selects the strongest signal to be repeated
   B. allows repeater users to make telephone calls from their stations
   C. locks other repeaters out of important, confidential communications
   D. connects a mobile station to the next repeater if it moves out of range

3. Which of the following is NOT an advantage gained by using a crystal in radio equipment?   3._____
   Increased

   A. power generation   B. frequency stability
   C. overtone generation   D. frequency accuracy

4. The purpose of a key-operated on/off switch in the main power line of a station is to   4._____

   A. keep the power company from shutting down power during an emergency
   B. protect against failure of the main fuses
   C. turn off the station in the event of an emergency
   D. keep unauthorized persons from using the station

5. For two-way systems situated in and around an urban area, what block of frequencies are allocated for use by citizen two-way users? _____ MHz.   5._____

   A. 30   B. 40   C. 470-512   D. 900

6. A reactance tube is used to develop a(n) _____ signal.   6._____

   A. drift-free AM   B. FM
   C. SSB   D. TTY

7. Messages concerning a person's well-being that are sent into or out of a disaster area are _____ traffic messages.   7._____

   A. routine   B. tactical
   C. formal message   D. health and welfare

8. A(n) _____ is used to measure standing wave ratio.   8._____

   A. SWR meter   B. current bridge
   C. ammeter   D. ohmmeter

43

9. What is the USUAL remedy for an FM hand-held transceiver that is over-deviating?

   A. Talk more loudly into the microphone
   B. Change to a higher power level
   C. Talk farther from the microphone
   D. Allow the transceiver to cool

10. *Backwave radiation* is radiation

    A. from the rear of the antenna
    B. leaking from a CW antenna
    C. from a CW transmitter with the key open
    D. from a phone transmitter during silent periods

11. The input impedance of a grounded-grid amplifer is

    A. low   B. moderate   C. high   D. very high

12. If a dial which reads 4.525 MHz were marked in kilohertz, it would read _____ kHz.

    A. 4,525,000   B. 4525   C. .004525   D. 45.25

13. A _____ system uses a total of three transmission frequencies.

    A. simplex   B. duplex   C. repeater   D. remote

14. The basic unit of frequency is the

    A. hertz   B. ohm
    C. ampere   D. wave ratio

15. What type of feedback is required for an oscillator?

    A. Split-phase   B. In-phase
    C. Grid-leak   D. Degenerative

16. Cross-band operation of a repeater station is

    A. permitted, but requires a special state license
    B. permitted under the regular repeater station license
    C. permitted if the repeater receives signals in both bands
    D. not permitted under any circumstances

17. If an unlicensed third party is allowed to use your station, what must you do at your center of operations?

    A. Monitor and supervise the third party's participation when communication occurs at below 30 MHz.
    B. Continuously monitor and supervise the third party's participation.
    C. Key the transmitter and make the station identification.
    D. Report the third party to the FCC.

18. Receive overload is caused by

    A. too much voltage from the power supply
    B. interference from a poorly-adjusted volume control
    C. too much current from the power supply
    D. interference from the signals of a nearby transmitter

18.____

19. Equal but opposite signals are required for operating a _____ amplifier.

    A. parallel   B. push-pull   C. class C   D. series

19.____

20. The MAIN purpose of shielding a transmitter is to

    A. prevent unwanted radio-frequency radiation
    B. keep electronic parts warmer and more stable
    C. give low-pass air filter a solid support
    D. help the sound quality

20.____

21. In an FM signal, whether modulated or unmodulated, the

    A. carrier frequency amplitude is fixed
    B. modulating frequency varies
    C. carrier frequency varies
    D. modulating frequency is fixed

21.____

22. For voice operation, the microphone is connected to the

    A. antenna switch   B. transceiver
    C. power supply   D. antenna

22.____

23. Harmonic radiation is unwanted signals

    A. that are combined with a 60-Hz hum
    B. caused by vibrations from a nearby transmitter
    C. at frequencies which are multiples of an operator's chosen frequency
    D. which cause skip propagation

23.____

24. The LOWEST frequency of electrical energy that is usually known as radio frequency is _____ Hz.

    A. 20   B. 2,000   C. 20,000   D. 200,000

24.____

25. What is the term for the kind of interference created by a continuous broad band of numerous unrelated radio frequency pulses?

    A. Chirp   B. Oscillation
    C. Impulse noise   D. Fluctuation noise

25.____

4 (#2)

KEY (CORRECT ANSWERS)

1.	D	11.	A
2.	B	12.	B
3.	A	13.	B
4.	D	14.	A
5.	C	15.	B
6.	B	16.	D
7.	D	17.	B
8.	A	18.	D
9.	C	19.	B
10.	C	20.	A

21. C
22. B
23. C
24. C
25. D

EXAMINATION SECTION
TEST 1

DIRECTIONS: Each question or incomplete statement is followed by several suggested answers or completions. Select the one that BEST answers the question or completes the statement. *PRINT THE LETTER OF THE CORRECT ANSWER IN THE SPACE AT THE RIGHT.*

1. When a signal report is referred to as *five nine plus 10 db,* 1.____

    A. its bandwidth is 10 decibels above linearity
    B. its relative signal strength reading is 10 decibels greater than strength 9
    C. its signal strength has increased by a factor of 90
    D. it should be repeated at a frequency 10 kHz higher

2. *Chirp* is a(n) 2.____

    A. overload in a receiver's audio circuit whenever CW is received
    B. slight change in a transmitter's frequency each time it is keyed
    C. gradual change in transmitter frequency as the circuit warms up
    D. high-pitched tone received with a CW signal

3. A vertical antenna sends out MOST of its radio energy 3.____

    A. in two opposite directions
    B. high into the air
    C. equally in all horizontal directions
    D. in one direction

4. For correct station identification when using a radiotelephone, FCC rules suggest using _____ as an aid. 4.____

    A. a phonetic alphabet
    B. unique words of the operator's choice
    C. Q signals
    D. a speech compressor

5. A COMMON result of an operator speaking too loudly into a hand-held FM transceiver is 5.____

    A. interference to other stations operating near the operator's frequency
    B. digital interference to computer equipment
    C. atmospheric interference in the air around the antenna
    D. interference to stations operating on a higher frequency band

6. When using a repeater to transmit a two-way radio signal, the operator should pause briefly between transmissions to 6.____

    A. dial up the repeater's autopatch
    B. listen for anyone wanting to break in
    C. prepare for recording possible third-party communications
    D. check the standing-wave ratio of the repeater

7. The USUAL input/output frequency separation for repeaters in the 2-meter band is

   A. 1 MHz B. 5 MHz C. 1.5 MHz D. 600 kHz

8. What is the PROPER way to ask someone's location when using a repeater?

   A. What is your QTH? B. What is your 20?
   C. Where are you? D. Where's the break?

9. If an ammeter reads 4 amperes, the current flow, in milliamperes, is

   A. .004 B. 4,000,000 C. 4000 D. .0004

10. The purpose of repeater operation is to

    A. cut power costs by linking with another high-power system
    B. help mobile and low-power stations extend their ranges
    C. transmit signals for observing propagation and reception
    D. make calls within a range of 50 miles

11. For two-way systems situated in and around an urban area, what block of frequencies are allocated for use by police, fire, and private industries? _____ MHz.

    A. 30 B. 40 C. 470-512 D. 900

12. What causes the MAXIMUM usable frequency to vary?

    A. The amount of ultraviolet radiation from the sun
    B. Windspeed in the upper atmosphere
    C. The temperature of the ionosphere
    D. The weather just below the ionosphere

13. A transmission line that has no change in voltage or current along its full length has a standing-wave ratio of

    A. less than 1 B. greater than 1
    C. 1:1 D. 2:1

14. When a signal is referred to as *full quieting*, it

    A. is not strong enough to be received
    B. is being received, but no audio is being heard
    C. contains no extraneous sound
    D. is strong enough to overcome all receiver noise

15. During transmission, the antenna of a hand-held transceiver should be held pointing

    A. toward the ground
    B. away from the operator's head and away from others
    C. toward the station the operator means to contact
    D. away from the station the operator means to contact

16. A _____ system is MOST at risk of receiving a barrage of calls from different sources at the same time.

    A. duplex B. simplex C. repeater D. remote

17. The device that measures standing wave ratio should be connected between the   17.____
    A. transmitter and power supply
    B. ground and transmitter
    C. feed line and antenna
    D. receiver and transmitter

18. Electrical energy at a frequency of 7120 Hz is in the _____ frequency range.   18.____
    A. hyper   B. audio
    C. super-high   D. radio

19. The type of system in which the transmitter and receiver are at a different location from   19.____
    the microphone and loudspeaker is the _____ system.
    A. remote   B. repeater   C. simplex   D. duplex

20. In the radio transmission of speech, the amplification added to a signal to prevent degra-   20.____
    dation of consonant sounds is referred to as
    A. preemphasis   B. deemphasis
    C. loading   D. squelch

21. The bandwidth over which a receiver is capable of receiving signals is referred to as its   21.____
    A. monitor band   B. sideband
    C. skip zone   D. acceptance band

22. The output of a transceiver should NEVER be connected to a(n)   22.____
    A. antenna switch   B. receiver
    C. SWR meter   D. antenna

23. Which band may NOT be used by earth stations for satellite communications?   23.____
    A. 10 meters   B. 6 meters
    C. 2 meters   D. 70 centimeters

24. What is the term for the kind of interference created by sharp bursts of radio frequency   24.____
    voltage?
    A. Chirp   B. Oscillation
    C. Impulse noise   D. Fluctuation noise

25. In repeater operations, a courtesy tone   25.____
    A. indicates a waiting message
    B. activates a receiver in case of severe weather
    C. identifies the repeater
    D. indicates that the transmission has been completed

KEY (CORRECT ANSWERS)

1. B
2. B
3. C
4. A
5. A

6. B
7. D
8. C
9. C
10. B

11. A
12. A
13. C
14. D
15. B

16. B
17. C
18. D
19. A
20. A

21. D
22. B
23. B
24. C
25. D

TEST 2

DIRECTIONS: Each question or incomplete statement is followed by several suggested answers or completions. Select the one that BEST answers the question or completes the statement. *PRINT THE LETTER OF THE CORRECT ANSWER IN THE SPACE AT THE RIGHT.*

1. Maximum usable frequency means the _____ frequency signal that _____.   1._____

    A. highest; is most absorbed by the ionosphere
    B. lowest; is most absorbed by the ionosphere
    C. lowest; will reach its intended destination
    D. highest; will reach its intended destination

2. As its wavelength gets LONGER, a signal's frequency   2._____

    A. lengthens   B. shortens
    C. stays the same   D. disappears

3. The term for voice emissions that are radio-transmitted is   3._____

    A. RTTY   B. CW   C. data   D. phone

4. A _____ is used to inject a frequency calibration signal into a receiver.   4._____

    A. calibrated voltmeter   B. calibrated wavemeter
    C. crystal calibrator   D. calibrated oscilloscope

5. The basic unit of electric current is the   5._____

    A. volt   B. ampere   C. watt   D. ohm

6. An amateur radiotelephone station operated as a mobile station is identified by   6._____

    A. transmitting the word *mobile* after the call sign
    B. at the end of every ten minutes, transmitting the call sign followed by the word *mobile*
    C. after the call sign, transmitting the word *mobile,* followed by the call sign area in which the station is operating
    D. transmitting the area of operation after the call sign

7. Which type of repeater operation should be DISCOURAGED during commuter rush hours?   7._____

    A. Traffic information networks
    B. Low-power stations
    C. Mobile stations
    D. Third-party networks

8. The MOST effective way of checking the accuracy of a receiver's tuning dial would be to tune to   8._____

    A. one of the frequencies of station WWV or WWVH
    B. a popular amateur network frequency
    C. the frequency of a shortwave broadcasting station
    D. an amateur station and ask what frequency the operator is using

9. A(n) _____ produces a stable, low-level signal that can be set to a desired frequency.

   A. oscilloscope
   B. reflectometer
   C. signal generator
   D. wavemeter

10. What is the PROPER distress call to use when operating continuous-wave?

    A. MAYDAY   B. HELP   C. QRZ   D. SOS

11. What device should be connected to a transmitter's output when an operator is making transmitter adjustments?

    A. Dummy antenna
    B. Reflectometer
    C. Receiver
    D. Multimeter

12. The BEST way to minimize on-air interference during a lengthy transmitter test procedure is by

    A. using a resonant antenna that requires no loading-up
    B. using a dummy load
    C. using a non-resonant antenna
    D. choosing an unoccupied frequency

13. At what point in an operator's station is the transceiver power measured?

    A. At the power supply terminals
    B. At the antenna terminals
    C. On the antenna
    D. At the final amplifier input terminals

14. A(n) _____ meter is used to measure relative signal strength in a receiver.

    A. RST
    B. signal deviation
    C. S
    D. SSB

15. When a signal is referred to as *five seven*, it is

    A. perfectly readable, but weak
    B. readable with considerable difficulty
    C. perfectly readable and moderately strong
    D. readable with a nearly pure tone

16. What is the result of overdeviation in an FM transmitter?

    A. Increased transmitter power
    B. Out-of-channel emissions
    C. Increased transmitter range
    D. Poor carrier suppression

17. For safety, the BEST thing to do with transmitting antennas is

    A. use vertical polarization
    B. use horizontal polarization
    C. mount them close to the ground
    D. mount them where nobody can come near them

18. _____ may be caused by a multi-band antenna connected to a poorly-tuned antenna.

    A. Auroral distortion
    B. Parasitic excitation
    C. Harmonic radiation
    D. Intermodulation

19. Using a final amplifier capable of providing a 100 W output to a transmission line that provides a 10-decibel loss, the antenna will receive _____ W of power.

    A. 1   B. 10   C. 90   D. 100

20. For two-way systems situated in and around an urban area, what block of frequencies are allocated for use by land mobile services? _____ MHz.

    A. 30   B. 40   C. 470-512   D. 900

21. What type of messages are sent into or out of a disaster area and concern the immediate safety of human life? _____ traffic.

    A. Emergency
    B. Tactical
    C. Formal message
    D. Health and welfare

22. 50 hertz means 50

    A. meters per second
    B. cycles per meter
    C. cycles per second
    D. cycles per minute

23. A common result of operating an FM transmitter with the microphone gain set too high is

    A. atmospheric interference in the air around the antenna
    B. digital interference to computer equipment
    C. interference to other stations operating near the operator's frequency
    D. interference to stations operating on a higher frequency band

24. Which is the SIMPLEST type of system for which simultaneous transmission and reception are possible?

    A. Remote   B. Repeater   C. Duplex   D. Simplex

25. *Splatter interference* is caused by

    A. overmodulation of a transmitter
    B. keying a transmitter too quickly
    C. routing of a transmitter's output signals back to its input circuit
    D. a transmitting antenna of the wrong length

KEY (CORRECT ANSWERS)

1. D
2. B
3. D
4. C
5. B

6. C
7. D
8. A
9. C
10. D

11. A
12. B
13. B
14. C
15. C

16. B
17. D
18. C
19. B
20. D

21. A
22. C
23. C
24. B
25. A

MAP READING
EXAMINATION SECTION
TEST 1

DIRECTIONS: Each question or incomplete statement is followed by several suggested answers or completions. Select the one that BEST answers the question or completes the Statement. *PRINT THE LETTER OF THE CORRECT ANSWER IN THE SPACE AT THE RIGHT.*

Questions 1-5.

DIRECTIONS: Questions 1 through 5 are to be answered SOLELY on the basis of the following information and map.

An employee may be required to assist civilians who seek travel directions or referral to city agencies and facilities.

The following is a map of part of a city, where several public offices and other institutions are located. Each of the squares represents one city block. Street names are as shown. If there is an arrow next to the street name, it means the street is one-way only in the direction of the arrow. If there is no arrow next to the street name, two-way traffic is allowed.

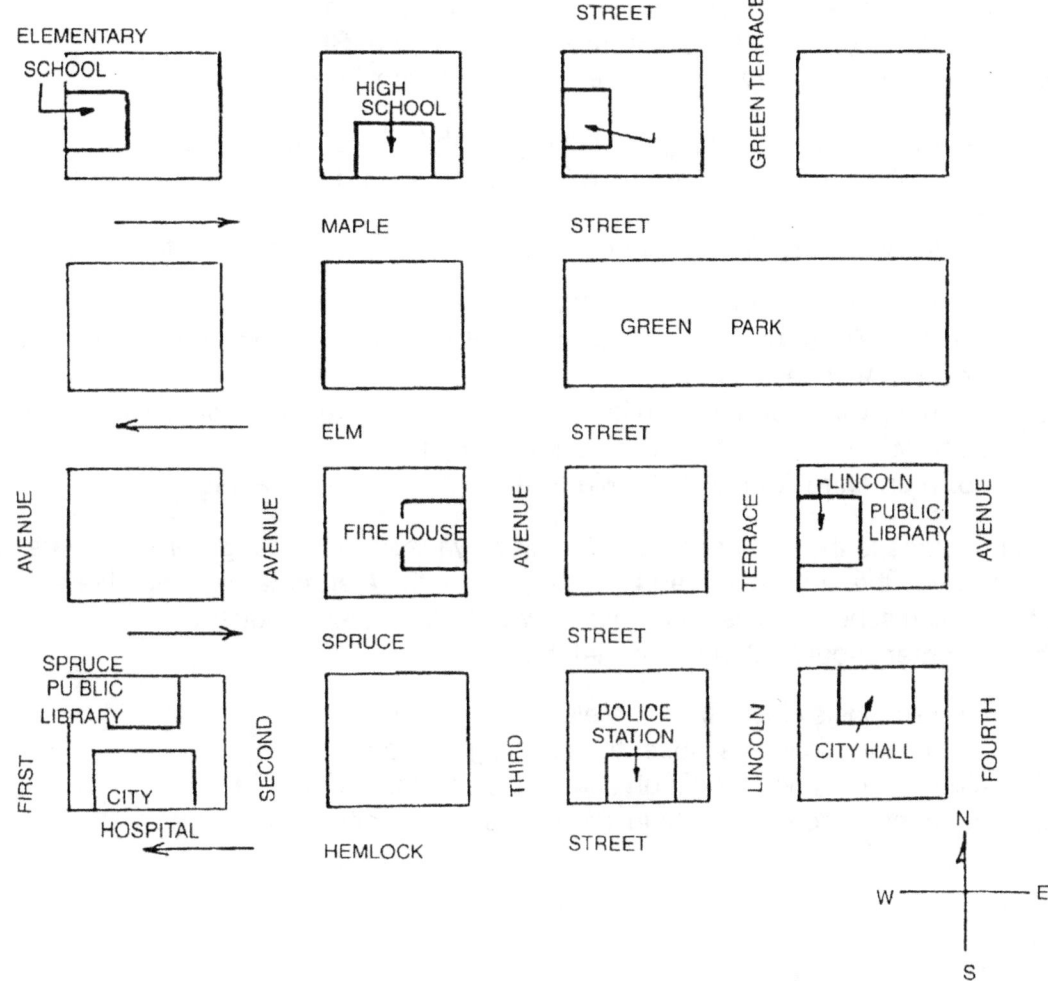

55

1. A woman whose handbag was stolen from her in Green Park asks a firefighter at the firehouse where to go to report the crime.
   The firefighter should tell the woman to go to the

   A. police station on Spruce Street
   B. police station on Hemlock Street
   C. city hall on Spruce Street
   D. city hall on Hemlock Street

1. ___

2. A disabled senior citizen who lives on Green Terrace telephones the firehouse to ask which library is closest to her home.
   The firefighter should tell the senior citizen it is the

   A. Spruce Public Library on Lincoln Terrace
   B. Lincoln Public Library on Spruce Street
   C. Spruce Public Library on Spruce Street
   D. Lincoln Public Library on Lincoln Terrace

2. ___

3. A woman calls the firehouse to ask for the exact location of City Hall.
   She should be told that it is on

   A. Hemlock Street, between Lincoln Terrace and Fourth Avenue
   B. Spruce Street, between Lincoln Terrace and Fourth Avenue
   C. Lincoln Terrace, between Spruce Street and Elm Street
   D. Green Terrace, between Maple Street and Pine Street

3. ___

4. A delivery truck driver is having trouble finding the high school to make a delivery. The driver parks the truck across from the firehouse on Third Avenue facing north and goes into the firehouse to ask directions.
   In giving directions, the firefighter should tell the driver to go _____ to the school.

   A. north on Third Avenue to Pine Street and then make a right
   B. south on Third Avenue, make a left on Hemlock Street, and then make a right on Second Avenue
   C. north on Third Avenue, turn left on Elm Street, make a right on Second Avenue and go to Maple Street, then make another right
   D. north on Third Avenue to Maple Street, and then make a left

4. ___

5. A man comes to the firehouse accompanied by his son and daughter. He wants to register his son in the high school and his daughter in the elementary school. He asks a firefighter which school is closest for him to walk to from the firehouse.
   The firefighter should tell the man that the

   A. high school is closer than the elementary school
   B. elementary school is closer than the high school
   C. elementary school and high school are the same distance away
   D. elementary school and high school are in opposite directions

5. ___

Questions 6-8.

DIRECTIONS: Questions 6 through 8 are to be answered SOLELY on the basis of the following map and information. The flow of traffic is indicated by the arrows. If there is only one arrow shown, then traffic flows in the direction indicated by the arrow. If there are two arrows, then traffic flows in both directions. You must follow the flow of traffic

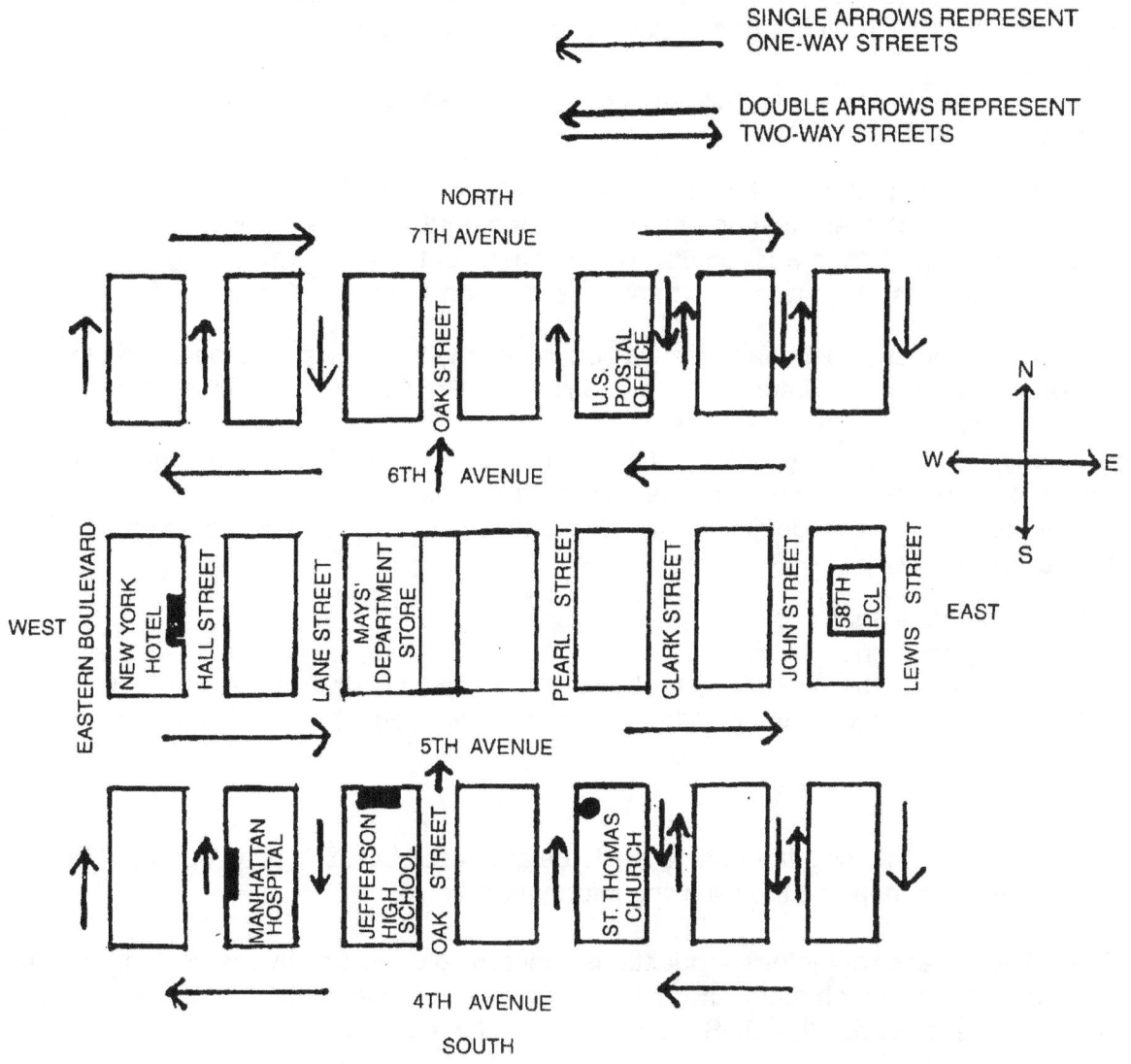

6. Traffic Enforcement Agent Fox was on foot patrol at John Street between 6th and 7th Avenues when a motorist driving southbound asked her for directions to the New York Hotel, which is located on Hall Street between 5th and 6th Avenues. Which one of the following is the SHORTEST route for Agent Fox to direct the motorist to take, making sure to obey all traffic regulations?
Travel _____ to the New York Hotel.

   A. north on John Street, then east on 7th Avenue, then north on Lewis Street, then west on 4th Avenue, then north on Eastern Boulevard, then east on 5th Avenue, then north on Hall Street
   B. south on John Street, then west on 6th Avenue, then south on Eastern Boulevard, then east on 5th Avenue, then north on Hall Street

C. south on John Street, then west on 6th Avenue, then south on Clark Street, then east on 4th Avenue, then north on Eastern Boulevard, then east on 5th Avenue, then north on Hall Street
D. south on John Street, then west on 4th Avenue, then north on Hall Street

7. Traffic Enforcement Agent Murphy is on motorized patrol on 7th Avenue between Oak Street and Pearl Street when Lt. Robertson radios him to go to Jefferson High School, located on 5th Avenue between Lane Street and Oak Street. Which one of the following is the SHORTEST route for Agent Murphy to take, making sure to obey all the traffic regulations?
Travel east on 7th Avenue, then south on _____, then east on 5th Avenue to Jefferson High School.

   A. Clark Street, then west on 4th Avenue, then north on Hall Street
   B. Pearl Street, then west on 4th Avenue, then north on Lane Street
   C. Lewis Street, then west on 6th Avenue, then south on Hall Street
   D. Lewis Street, then west on 4th Avenue, then north on Oak Street

8. Traffic Enforcement Agent Vasquez was on 4th Avenue and Eastern Boulevard when a motorist asked him for directions to the 58th Police Precinct, which is located on Lewis Street between 5th and 6th Avenues.
Which one of the following is the SHORTEST route for Agent Vasquez to direct the motorist to take, making sure to obey all traffic regulations.
Travel north on Eastern Boulevard, then east on _____ on Lewis Street to the 58th Police Precinct.

   A. 5th Avenue, then north
   B. 7th Avenue, then south
   C. 6th Avenue, then north on Pearl Street, then east on 7th Avenue, then south
   D. 5th Avenue, then north on Clark Street, then east on 6th Avenue, then south

Questions 9-13.

DIRECTIONS: Questions 9 through 13 are to be answered SOLELY on the basis of the following map and the following information.

Toll collectors answer motorists' questions concerning directions by reading a map of the metropolitan area. Although many alternate routes leading to destinations exist on the following map, you are to choose the MOST direct route of those given.

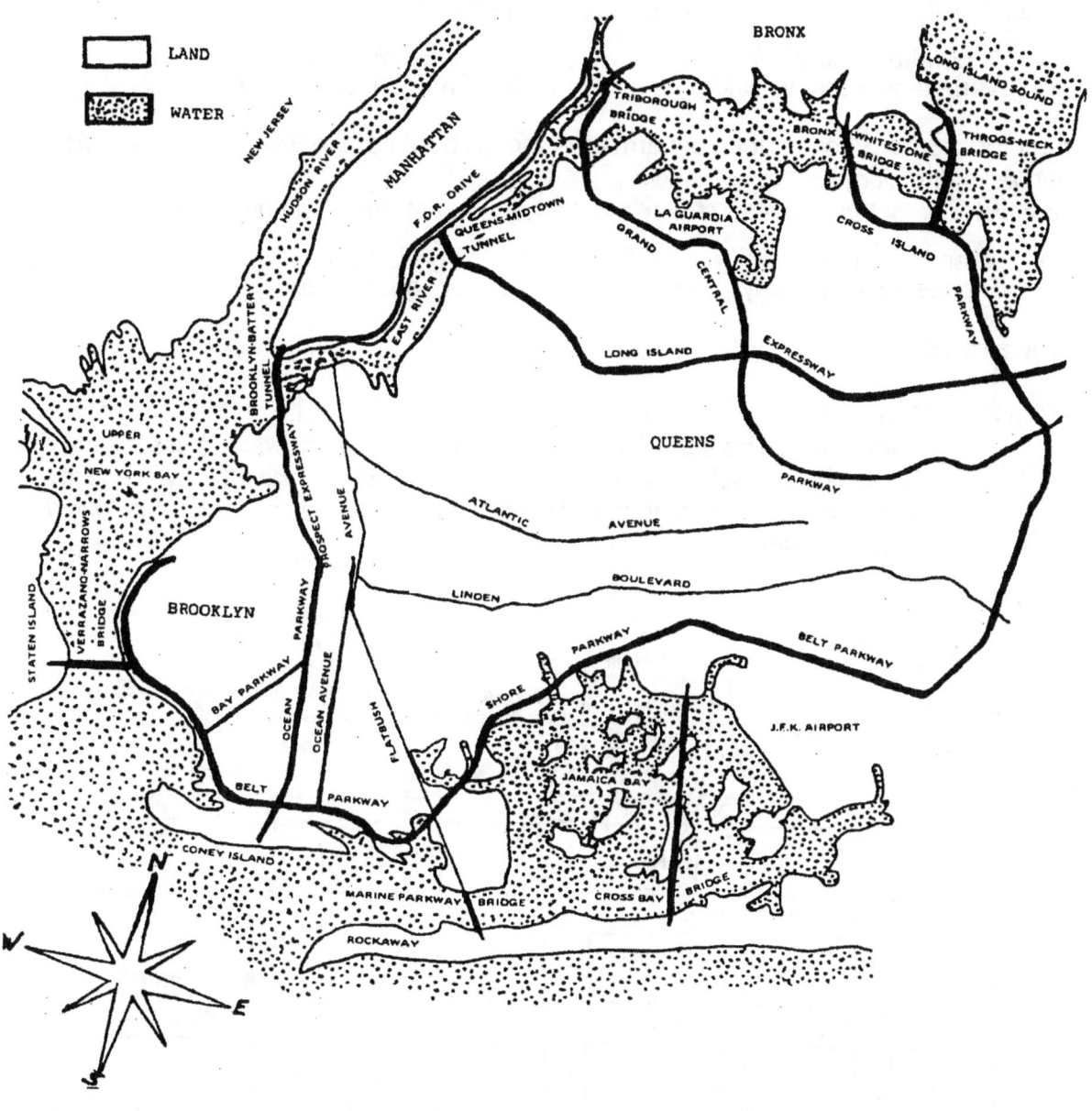

9. A motorist driving from the Bronx over the Triborough Bridge wants to go to LaGuardia Airport in Queens.
   The officer should direct him to

   A. Grand Central Parkway
   B. F.D.R. Drive
   C. Shore Parkway
   D. Flatbush Avenue

10. A motorist driving from Manhattan through the Queens Midtown Tunnel would travel DIRECTLY onto

   A. Shore Parkway
   B. F.D.R. Drive
   C. Long Island Expressway
   D. Atlantic Avenue

11. A motorist traveling north over the Marine Parkway Bridge should take which route to reach Coney Island?

   A. Shore Parkway East
   B. Belt Parkway West
   C. Linden Boulevard
   D. Ocean Parkway

12. Which facility does NOT connect the Bronx and Queens?

    A. Triborough Bridge
    B. Bronx-Whitestone Bridge
    C. Verrazano-Narrows Bridge
    D. Throgs-Neck Bridge

13. A motorist driving from Manhattan arrives at the toll booth of the Brooklyn-Battery Tunnel and asks directions to Ocean Parkway.
    To which one of the following routes should the motorist FIRST be directed?

    A. Atlantic Avenue
    B. Bay Parkway
    C. Prospect Expressway
    D. Ocean Avenue

Questions 14-16.

DIRECTIONS: Questions 14 through 16 are to be answered SOLELY on the basis of the following map. The flow of traffic is indicated by the arrows. If there is only one arrow shown, then traffic flows only in the direction indicated by the arrow. If there are two arrows, then traffic flows in both directions. You must follow the flow of traffic.

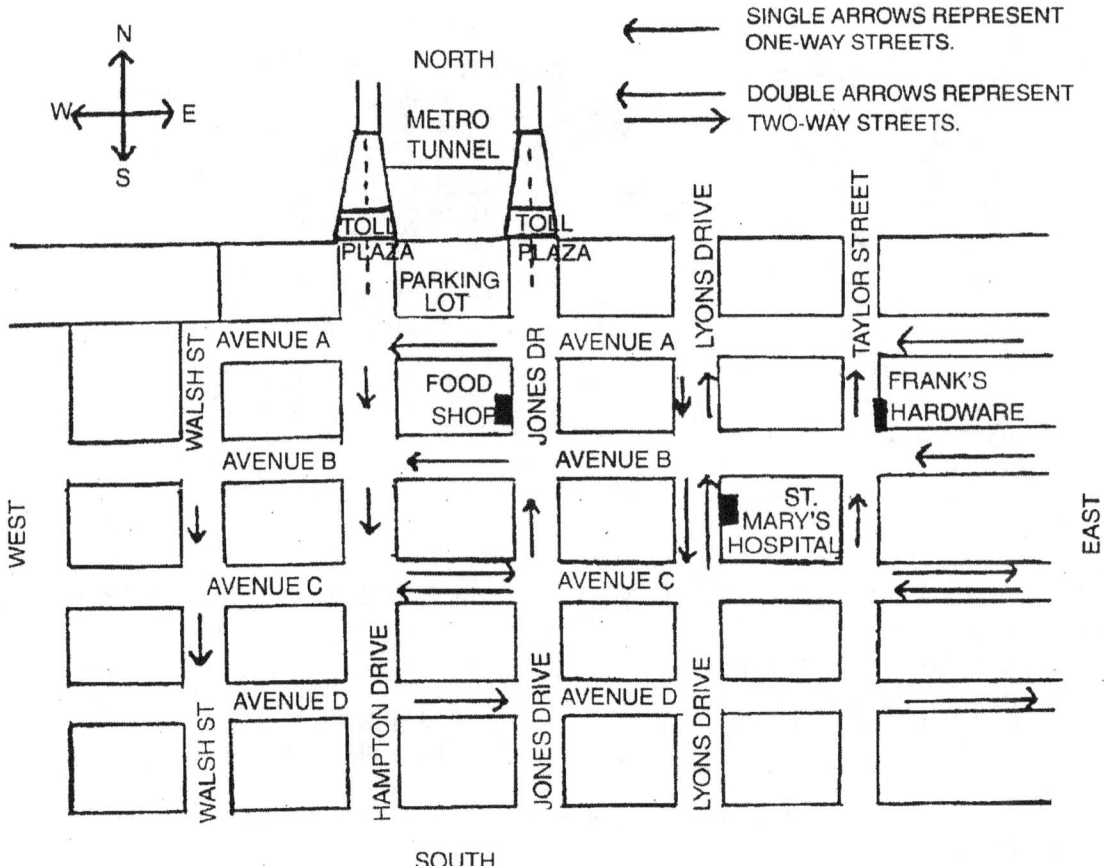

14. A motorist is exiting the Metro Tunnel and approaches the bridge and tunnel officer at the toll plaza. He asks the officer how to get to the food shop on Jones Drive. Which one of the following is the SHORTEST route for the motorist to take, making sure to obey all traffic regulations?
    Travel south on Hampton Drive, then left on _____ on Jones Drive to the food shop.

A. Avenue A, then right
B. Avenue B, then right
C. Avenue D, then left
D. Avenue C, then left

15. A motorist heading south pulls up to a toll booth at the exit of the Metro Tunnel and asks Bridge and Tunnel Officer Evans how to get to Frank's Hardware Store on Taylor Street. Which one of the following is the SHORTEST route for the motorist to take, making sure to obey all traffic regulations?
Travel south on Hampton Drive, then east on

15.____

A. Avenue B to Taylor Street
B. Avenue D, then north on Taylor Street to Avenue B
C. Avenue C, then north on Taylor Street to Avenue B
D. Avenue C, then north on Lyons Drive, then east on Avenue B to Taylor Street

16. A motorist is exiting the Metro Tunnel and approaches the toll plaza. She asks Bridge and Tunnel Officer Owens for directions to St. Mary's Hospital. Which one of the following is the SHORTEST route for the motorist to take, making sure to obey all traffic regulations?
Travel south on Hampton Drive, then _____ on Lyons Drive to St. Mary's Hospital.

16.____

A. left on Avenue D, then left
B. right on Avenue A, then left on Walsh Street, then left on Avenue D, then left
C. left on Avenue C, then left
D. left on Avenue B, then right

Questions 17-18.

DIRECTIONS: Questions 17 and 18 are to be answered SOLELY on the basis of the map which appears on the following page. The flow of traffic is indicated by the arrows. If there is only one arrow shown, then traffic flows only in the direction indicated by the arrow. If there are two arrows shown, then traffic flows in both directions. You must follow the flow of traffic.

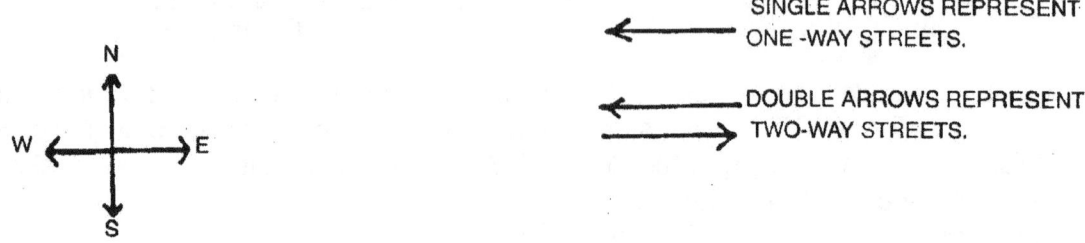

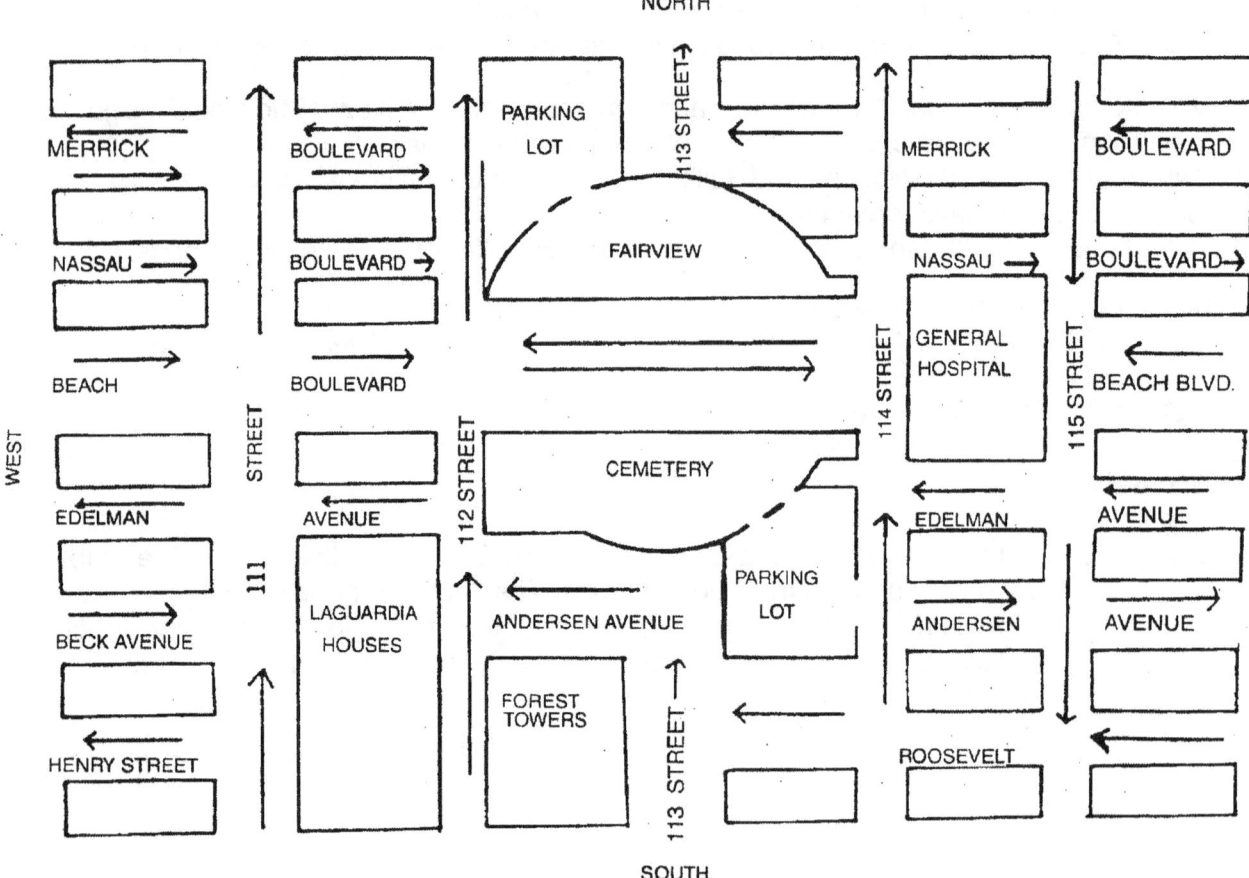

17. Police Officers Glenn and Albertson are on 111th Street at Henry Street when they are dispatched to a past robbery at Beach Boulevard and 115th Street.
Which one of the following is the SHORTEST route for the officers to follow in their patrol car, making sure to obey all traffic regulations?
Travel north on 111th Street, then east on _____ south on 115th Street.

   A. Edelman Avenue, then north on 112th Street, then east on Beach Boulevard, then north on 114th Street, then east on Nassau Boulevard, then one block
   B. Beach Boulevard, then north on 114th Street, then east on Nassau Boulevard, then one block
   C. Merrick Boulevard, then two blocks
   D. Nassau Boulevard, then south on 112th Street, then east on Beach Boulevard, then north on 114th Street, then east on Nassau Boulevard, then one block

18. Later in their tour, Officers Glenn and Albertson are driving on 114th Street. If they make a left turn to enter the parking lot at Andersen Avenue, and then make a u-turn, in what direction would they now be headed?

    A. North   B. South   C. East   D. West

Questions 19-20.

DIRECTIONS: Questions 19 and 20 are to be answered SOLELY on the basis of the following map. The flow of traffic is indicated by the arrows. If there is only one arrow shown, then traffic flows only in the direction indicated by the arrow. If there are two arrows shown, then traffic flows in both directions. You must follow the flow of traffic.

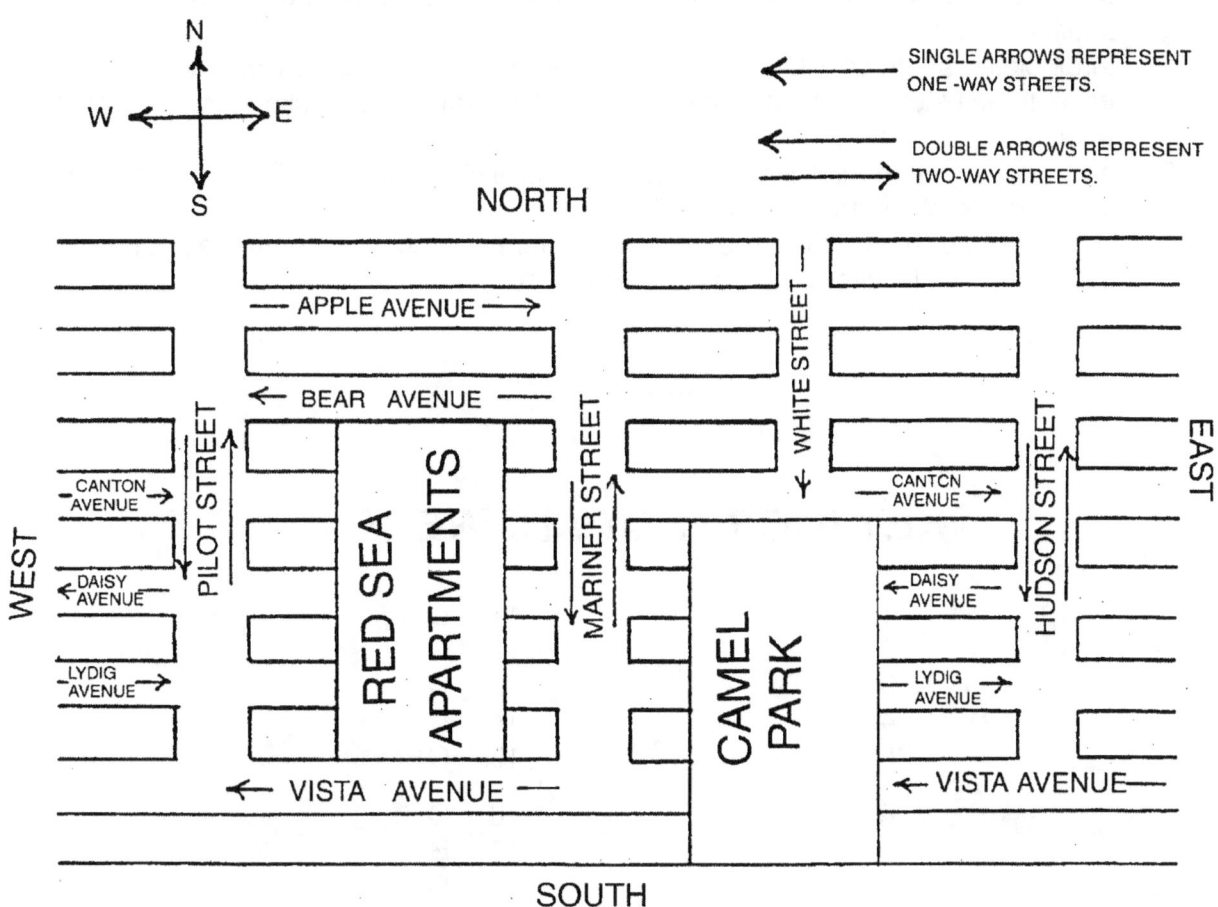

19. You are located at Apple Avenue and White Street. You receive a call to respond to the corner of Lydig Avenue and Pilot Street.
    Which one of the following is the MOST direct route for you to take in your patrol car, making sure to obey all traffic regulations?
    Travel _____ on Pilot Street.

    A. two blocks south on White Street, then one block east on Canton Avenue, then one block north on Hudson Street, then three blocks west on Bear Avenue, then three blocks south
    B. one block south on White Street, then two blocks west on Bear Avenue, then three blocks south

C. two blocks west on Apple Avenue, then four blocks south
D. two blocks south on White Street, then one block west on Canton Avenue, then three blocks south on Mariner Street, then one block west on Vista Avenue, then one block north

20. You are located at Canton Avenue and Pilot Street. You receive a call of a crime in progress at the intersection of Canton Avenue and Hudson Street.
Which one of the following is the MOST direct route for you to take in your patrol car, making sure to obey all traffic regulations?
Travel

    A. two blocks north on Pilot Street, then two blocks east on Apple Avenue, then one block south on White Street, then one block east on Bear Avenue, then one block south on Hudson Street
    B. three blocks south on Pilot Street, then travel one block east on Vista Avenue, then travel three blocks north on Mariner Street, then travel two blocks east on Canton Avenue
    C. one block north on Pilot Street, then travel three blocks east on Bear Avenue, then travel one block south on Hudson Street
    D. two blocks north on Pilot Street, then travel three blocks east on Apple Avenue, then travel two blocks south on Hudson Street

20.____

KEY (CORRECT ANSWERS)

1. B
2. D
3. B
4. C
5. A

6. D
7. A
8. B
9. A
10. C

11. B/D
12. C
13. C
14. D
15. C

16. C
17. B
18. C
19. B
20. D

READING COMPREHENSION
UNDERSTANDING AND INTERPRETING WRITTEN MATERIAL

EXAMINATION SECTION
TEST 1

DIRECTIONS: Each question or incomplete statement is followed by several suggested answers or completions. Select the one that BEST answers the question or completes the statement. *PRINT THE LETTER OF THE CORRECT ANSWER IN THE SPACE AT THE RIGHT.*

Questions 1-4.

DIRECTIONS: Questions 1 through 4 are to be answered SOLELY on the basis of the following paragraph.

The canister-type gas mask consists of a tight-fitting face piece connected to a canister containing chemicals which filter toxic gases and smoke from otherwise breathable air. These masks are of value when used with due regard to the fact that two or three percent of gas in air is about the highest concentration that the chemicals in the canister will absorb and that these masks do not provide the oxygen which is necessary for the support of life. In general, if flame is visible, there is sufficient oxygen for firefighters although toxic gases may be present. Where there is heavy smoke and no flame, an oxygen deficiency may exist. Fatalities have occurred where filter-type canister masks have been used in attempting rescue from manholes, wells, basements, or other locations deficient in oxygen.

1. If the mask described above is used in an atmosphere containing oxygen, nitrogen, and carbon monoxide, we would expect the mask to remove from the air breathed

    A. the nitrogen only
    B. the carbon monoxide only
    C. the nitrogen and the carbon monoxide
    D. none of these gases

2. According to the above paragraph, when a fireman is wearing one of these masks at a fire where flame is visible, he can GENERALLY feel that as far as breathing is concerned, he is

    A. *safe*, since the mask will provide him with sufficient oxygen to live
    B. *unsafe*, unless the gas concentration is below 2 or 3 percent
    C. *safe*, provided the gas concentration is above 2 or 3 percent
    D. *unsafe*, since the mask will not provide him with sufficient oxygen to live

3. According to the above paragraph, fatalities have occurred to persons using this type gas mask in manholes, wells, and basements because

    A. the supply of oxygen provided by the mask ran out
    B. the air in those places did not contain enough oxygen to support life
    C. heavy smoke interfered with the operation of the mask
    D. the chemicals in the canister did not function properly

4. The following shorthand formula may be used to show, in general, the operation of the gas mask described in the above paragraph:
(Chemicals in canister) → (Air + gases) = Breathable Air.
The arrow in the formula, when expressed in words, means MOST NEARLY

   A. replace
   B. are changed into
   C. act upon
   D. give off

Questions 5-7.

DIRECTIONS: Questions 5 through 7 are to be answered SOLELY on the basis of the following paragraph.

The only openings permitted in fire partitions, except openings for ventilating ducts, shall be those required for doors. There shall be but one such door opening unless the provision of additional openings would not exceed in total width of all doorways 25 percent of the length of the wall. The minimum distance between openings shall be three feet. The maximum area for such a door opening shall be 80 square feet, except that such openings for the passage of motor trucks may be a maximum of 140 square feet.

5. According to the above paragraph, openings in fire partitions are permitted ONLY for

   A. doors
   B. doors and windows
   C. doors and ventilation ducts
   D. doors, windows, and ventilation ducts

6. In a fire partition 22 feet long and 10 feet high, the MAXIMUM number of doors 3 feet wide and 7 feet high is

   A. 1   B. 2   C. 3   D. 4

7.

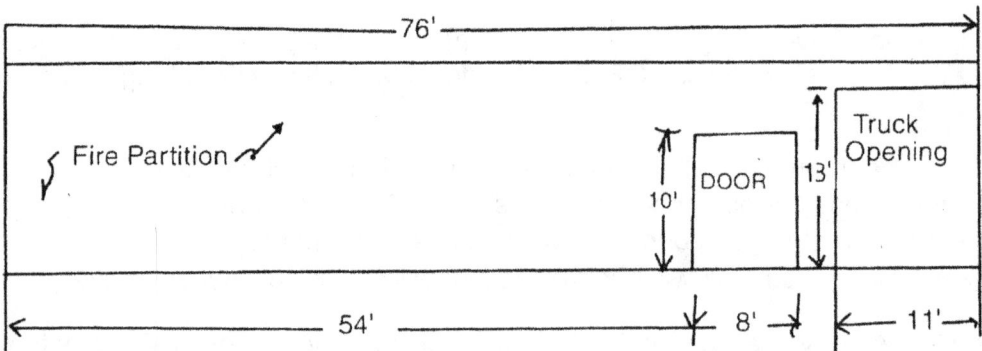

The one of the following statements about the layout shown above that is MOST accurate is that the

A. total width of the openings is too large
B. truck opening is too large
C. truck and door openings are too close together
D. layout is acceptable

Questions 8-11.

DIRECTIONS: Questions 8 through 11 are to be answered SOLELY on the basis of the following paragraph.

Division commanders shall arrange and maintain a plan for the use of hose wagons to transport members in emergencies. Upon receipt of a call for members, the deputy chief of the division from whom the men are called shall have the designated hose wagon placed out of service and prepared for the transportation of members. Hose wagons shall be placed at central assembly points, and members detailed instructed to report promptly to such locations equipped for fire duty. Hose wagons designated shall remain at regular assignments when not engaged in the transportation of members.

8. Preparation of the hose wagon for this special assignment of transporting of members would MOST likely involve

    A. checking the gas and oil, air in tires, and mechanical operation of the apparatus
    B. removal of hose lines to make room for the members being transported
    C. gathering of equipment which will be needed by the members being transported
    D. instructing the driver on the best route to be used

8._____

9. Hose wagons used for emergency transportation of members are placed out of service because they are

    A. not available to respond to alarms in their own district
    B. more subject to mechanical breakdown while on emergency duty
    C. engaged in operations which are not the primary responsibility of their division
    D. considered reserve equipment

9._____

10. Of the following, the BEST example of the type of emergency referred to in the above paragraph is a(n)

    A. fireman injured at a fire and requiring transportation
    B. subway strike which prevents firemen from reporting for duty
    C. unusually large number of false alarms occurring at one time
    D. need for additional manpower at a fire

10._____

11. A *central assembly point*, as used in the above paragraph, would MOST likely be a place

    A. close to the place of the emergency
    B. in the geographical center of the division
    C. easily reached by the members assigned
    D. readily accessible to the intersection of major highways

11._____

Questions 12-14.

DIRECTIONS: Questions 12 through 14 are to be answered SOLELY on the basis of the following paragraph.

A plastic does not consist of a single substance, but is a blended combination of several. In addition to the resin, it may contain various fillers, plasticizers, lubricants, and coloring material. Depending upon the type and quantity of substances added to the binder, the properties, including combustibility, may be altered considerably. The flammability of plastics depends upon the composition and, as with other materials, upon their physical size and condition. Thin sections, sharp edges, or powdered plastics will ignite and burn more readily than the same amount of identical material in heavy sections with smooth surfaces.

12. The one of the following conclusions that is BEST supported by the above paragraph is that the flammability of plastics

    A. generally is high
    B. generally is moderate
    C. generally is low
    D. varies considerably

13. According to the above paragraph, *plastics* can BEST be described as

    A. a trade name
    B. the name of a specific product
    C. the name of a group of products which have some similar and some dissimilar properties
    D. the name of any substance which can be shaped or molded during the production process

14. According to the above paragraph, all plastics contain a

    A. resin
    B. resin and a filler
    C. resin, filler, and plasticizer
    D. resin, filler, plasticizer, lubricant, and coloring material

Questions 15-18.

DIRECTIONS: Questions 15 through 18 are to be answered SOLELY on the basis of the following paragraph.

To guard against overheating of electrical conductors in buildings, an overcurrent protective device is provided for each circuit. This device is designed to open the circuit and cut off the flow of current whenever the current exceeds a predetermined limit. The fuse, which is the most common form of overcurrent protection, consists of a fusible metal element which when heated by the current to a certain temperature melts and opens the circuit.

15. According to the above paragraph, a circuit which is NOT carrying an electric current is a(n)

    A. open circuit
    B. closed circuit
    C. circuit protected by a fuse
    D. circuit protected by an overcurrent protective device other than a fuse

16. As used in the above paragraph, the one of the following which is the BEST example of a *conductor* is a(n)

    A. metal table which comes in contact with a source of electricity
    B. storage battery generating electricity
    C. electrical wire carrying an electrical current
    D. dynamo converting mechanical energy into electrical energy

17. A fuse is NOT

    A. an overcurrent protective device
    B. the most common form of overcurrent protection
    C. dangerous because it allows such a strong flow of electricity that the wires carrying it may become heated enough to set fire to materials in contact with them
    D. a safety valve

18. According to the above paragraph, the MAXIMUM number of circuits that can be handled by a fuse box containing 6 fuses

    A. is 3
    B. is 6
    C. is 12
    D. cannot be determined from the information given in the above Paragraph

Questions 19-21.

DIRECTIONS: Questions 19 through 21 are to be answered SOLELY on the basis of the following paragraph.

Unlined linen hose is essentially a fabric tube made of closely woven linen yarn. Due to the natural characteristics of linen, very shortly after water is introduced, the threads swell after being wet, closing the minute spaces between them making the tube practically water tight. This type of hose tends to deteriorate rapidly if not thoroughly dried after use or if installed where it will be exposed to dampness or the weather. It is not ordinarily built to withstand frequent service or for use where the fabric will be subjected to chafing from rough or sharp surfaces.

19. Seepage of water through an unlined linen hose is observed when the water is first turned on.
    From the above paragraph, we may conclude that the seepage

    A. indicates that the hose is defective
    B. does not indicate that the hose is defective provided that the seepage is proportionate to the water pressure
    C. does not indicate that the hose is defective provided that the seepage is greatly reduced when the hose becomes thoroughly wet
    D. does not indicate that the hose is defective provided that the seepage takes place only at the surface of the hose

20. Unlined linen hose is MOST suitable for use

    A. as a garden hose
    B. on fire department apparatus
    C. as emergency fire equipment in buildings
    D. in fire department training schools

21. The use of unlined linen hose would be LEAST appropriate in a(n)

    A. outdoor lumber yard
    B. non-fireproof office building
    C. department store
    D. cosmetic manufacturing plant

Questions 22-25.

DIRECTIONS: Questions 22 through 25 are to be answered SOLELY on the basis of the following paragraph.

The velocity of moving water droplets decreases because of aerodynamic drag forces and gravitational effects. In the case of droplets of the sizes more favorable for fire extinguishment, these aerodynamic drag forces, opposing the motion of the droplets, are proportional to the square of the diameters of the droplets and to the square of their velocity. If the initial velocity of the droplets leaving the spray nozzles is resolved into a horizontal and vertical component, the aerodynamic drag affects the horizontal component, and both the aerodynamic drag and gravitation affect the vertical component. In still air, the horizontal velocity of a moving droplet approaches zero. The vertical velocity of the droplet approaches the terminal velocity of a free falling body, which is attained when the aerodynamic drag forces are in equilibrium with the weight of the droplet. The terminal velocity represents the lower limit of the relative velocity of water drops in air. From the standpoint of fire fighting, the absolute velocity of the moving drops is also important, since the horizontal component of the absolute velocity must be sufficient for the droplets to reach the heated area surrounding the fire, and to penetrate the updraft to the seat of the fire.

22. The one of the following forces which would contribute MOST to *aerodynamic drag forces*, as that term is used in the above paragraph, is

    A. friction   B. gravity   C. inertia   D. momentum

23. Assume that water droplets in one stream have four times the diameter and the same initial velocity as droplets in a second stream.
    From the above paragraph, we may conclude that the aerodynamic drag forces on the first stream, compared to the second, initially are _____ as much.

    A. twice   B. four times
    C. eight times   D. sixteen times

24. The horizontal velocity of a moving droplet approaches zero when the

    A. horizontal velocity approaches the terminal velocity of a free falling body
    B. square of the diameter of the droplet is proportional to the square of the velocity of the droplet
    C. vertical velocity is in equilibrium with the aerodynamic drag forces
    D. maximum horizontal reach of the stream is obtained

25. The relative velocity of water droplets is equal to the absolute velocity when
   A. aerodynamic drag forces are in equilibrium with the weight of the droplets
   B. the square of the diameter of the droplets is proportional to the square of the velocity
   C. the air through which the droplets pass is still
   D. the aerodynamic drag forces equal the gravitational effects on the droplets

---

KEY (CORRECT ANSWERS)

1. B
2. B
3. B
4. C
5. C
6. A
7. B
8. B
9. A
10. D
11. C
12. D
13. C
14. A
15. A
16. A
17. C
18. B
19. C
20. C
21. A
22. A
23. D
24. D
25. C

TEST 2

Questions 1-4.

DIRECTIONS: Questions 1 through 4 are to be answered SOLELY on the basis of the following paragraph.

During fire operations, all members shall be constantly alert to possibility of the crime of arson. In the event conditions indicate this possibility, the officer in command shall promptly notify the Fire Marshal. Unauthorized persons shall be prohibited from entering premises and actions of those authorized carefully noted. Members shall refrain from discussion of the fire and prevent disturbance of essential evidence. If necessary, the officer in command shall detail one or more members at location with information for the Fire Marshal upon his arrival.

1. From the above paragraph, it may be inferred that the reason for prohibiting unauthorized persons from entering the fire premises when arson is suspected is to prevent such persons from

    A. endangering themselves in the fire
    B. interfering with the firemen fighting the fire
    C. disturbing any evidence of arson
    D. committing acts of arson

2. The one of the following titles which BEST describes the subject matter of the above paragraph is

    A. TECHNIQUES OF ARSON DETECTION
    B. THE ROLE OF THE FIRE MARSHAL IN ARSON CASES
    C. FIRE SCENE PROCEDURES IN CASES OF SUSPECTED ARSON
    D. EVIDENCE IN ARSON INVESTIGATIONS

3. The one of the following statements that is MOST correct and complete is that the responsibility for detecting signs of arson at a fire belongs to the

    A. Fire Marshal
    B. Fire Marshal and officer in command
    C. Fire Marshal, officer in command, and any members detailed at location with information for the Fire Marshal
    D. members present at the scene of the fire regardless of their rank or position

4. From the above paragraph, it may be inferred that the Fire Marshal USUALLY arrives at the scene of a fire

    A. before the fire companies
    B. simultaneously with the fire companies
    C. immediately after the fire companies
    D. some time after the fire companies

Questions 5-8.

DIRECTIONS: Questions 5 through 8 are to be answered SOLELY on the basis of the following paragraph.

FIRES

The four types of fires are called Class A, Class B, Class C, and Class D. Examples of Class A fires are paper, cloth, or wood fires. The types of extinguishers used on Class A fires are foam, soda acid, or water. Class B fires are those in burning liquids. They require a smothering action for extinguishment. Carbon dioxide, dry chemical, vaporizing liquid, or foam are the types of extinguishers that are used on burning liquids. Electrical fires, such as in motors and switches, are Class C fires. A non-conducting extinguishing agent must be used for this kind of fire. Therefore, carbon dioxide, dry chemical, or vaporizing liquid extinguishers are used. Fires in motor vehicles are Class D fires; and carbon dioxide, dry chemical, or vaporizing liquid extinguishers should be used on them.

5. According to the information in the above paragraph, a fire in a can full of gasoline would be a Class _____ fire.

   A. D B. C C. B D. A

6. In the above paragraph, the extinguishers recommended are entirely the same for Class _____ and Class _____ fires.

   A. B; D B. C; D C. B; C D. A; B

7. According to the information in the above paragraph, a water extinguisher would MOST likely be suitable for use on which one of the following fires? A(n)

   A. fire in a truck engine
   B. fire in an electrical switch
   C. oil fire
   D. lumber fire

8. According to the information in the above paragraph, dry chemical

   A. should NOT be used on a burning liquid fire
   B. is a conducting extinguishing agent
   C. should NOT be used on a fire in a car
   D. smothers fires to put them out

Questions 9-10.

DIRECTIONS: Questions 9 and 10 are to be answered SOLELY on the basis of the following passage.

One of the greatest hazards to an industrial plant is fire. Consequently, a rigid system should be set up for periodic inspection of all types of fire protective equipment. Such inspections should include water tanks, sprinkler systems, standpipes, hose, fire plugs, extinguishers, and all other equipment used for fire protection. The schedule of inspections should be closely followed and an *accurate* record kept of each piece of equipment inspected and tested.

Along with this scheduled inspection, a careful survey should be made of new equipment needed. Recommendations should be made for replacement of defective and obsolete equipment, as well as the purchase of any additional equipment. As new processes and products are added to the manufacturing system, new fire hazards may be introduced that require individual treatment and possible special extinguishing devices. Plant inspection personnel should be sure to follow through.

Surveys should also include all means of egress from the building. Exits, stairs, fire towers, fire escapes, halls, fire alarm systems, emergency lighting systems, and places seldom used should be thoroughly inspected to determine their adequacy and readiness for emergency use.

9. Of the following titles, the one that BEST fits the above passage is

    A. NEW, USED, AND OLD FIRE PROTECTION EQUIPMENT
    B. MAINTENANCE OF FIRE PROTECTION EQUIPMENT
    C. INSPECTION OF FIRE PROTECTION EQUIPMENT
    D. OVERHAUL OF WORN OUT FIRE FIGHTING EQUIPMENT

10. As used in the above passage, the word *accurate* means

    A. exact   B. approximate   C. close   D. vague

Questions 11-15.

DIRECTIONS: Questions 11 through 15 are to be answered SOLELY on the basis of the following passage.

The sizes of living rooms shall meet the following requirements:

a. In each apartment, there shall be at least one living room containing at least 120 square feet of clear floor area, and every other living room except a kitchen shall contain at least 70 square feet of clear floor area.
b. Every living room which contains less than 80 square feet of clear floor area or which is located in the cellar or basement shall be at least 9 feet high and every other living room 8 feet high.

Apartments containing three or more rooms may have dining bays, which shall not exceed 55 square feet in floor surface area and shall not be deemed separate rooms or subject to the requirements for separate rooms. Every such dining bay shall be provided with at least one window containing an area at least one-eighth of the floor surface area of such dining bay.

11. The MINIMUM volume of a living room, other than a kitchen, which meets the minimum requirements of the above paragraph is one that measures _____ cubic feet.

    A. 70   B. 80   C. 630   D. 640

12. A builder proposes to construct an apartment house containing an apartment consisting of a kitchen which measures 10 feet by 6 feet, a room 12 feet by 12 feet, and one 11 feet by 7 feet.
This apartment

    A. does not comply with the requirements of the above paragraph
    B. complies with the requirements of the above paragraph provided that it is not located in the cellar or basement

C. complies with the requirements of the above paragraph provided that the height of the smaller rooms is at least 9 feet
D. may or may not comply with the requirements of the above paragraph, depending upon the clear floor area of the kitchen

13. The one of the following definitions of the term *living room* which is MOST in accord with its meaning in the above paragraph is   13.____

    A. a sitting room or parlor
    B. the largest room in an apartment
    C. a room used for living purposes
    D. any room in an apartment containing 120 square feet of clear floor Area

14. Assume that one room in a four-room apartment measures 20 feet by 10 feet and contains a dining bay 8 feet by 6 feet. According to the above passage, the dining bay MUST be provided with a window measuring AT LEAST _____ square feet.   14.____

    A. 6   B. 7   C. 25   D. 55

15. Kitchens, according to the above passage, are   15.____

    A. not considered *living rooms*
    B. considered *living rooms* and must, therefore, meet the height and area requirements of the paragraph
    C. considered *living rooms* but they need not meet either the height or area requirements of the paragraph
    D. considered *living rooms* but they need meet only the height requirements, not the area requirements, of the paragraph

Questions 16-20.

DIRECTIONS: Questions 16 through 20 are to be answered SOLELY on the basis of the following paragraph.

Cotton fabrics treated with the XYZ Process have features which make them far superior to any previously known flame-retardant-treated cotton fabrics. XYZ are glow resistant; when exposed to flames or intense heat form tough, pliable, and protective chars; are inert physiologically to persons handling or exposed to the fabric; are only slightly heavier than untreated fabrics; and are susceptible to further wet and dry finishing treatments. In addition, the treated fabrics exhibit little or no adverse change in feel, texture, and appearance, and are shrink-, rot-, and mildew-resistant. The treatment reduces strength only slightly. Finished fabrics have *easy care* properties in that they are wrinkle-resistant and dry rapidly.

16. It is MOST accurate to state that the author, in the above paragraph, presents   16.____

    A. facts but reaches no conclusion concerning the value of the process
    B. his conclusion concerning the value of the process and facts to support his conclusion
    C. his conclusion concerning the value of the process unsupported by facts
    D. neither facts nor conclusions, but merely describes the process

17. The one of the following articles for which the XYZ Process would be MOST suitable is 17.____

    A. nylon stockings
    B. woolen shirt
    C. silk tie
    D. cotton bedsheet

18. The one of the following aspects of the XYZ Process which is NOT discussed in the above paragraph is its effects on 18.____

    A. costs
    B. washability
    C. wearability
    D. the human body

19. The MAIN reason for treating a fabric with the XYZ Process is to 19.____

    A. prepare the fabric for other wet and dry finishing treatments
    B. render it shrink-, rot-, and mildew-resistant
    C. increase its weight and strength
    D. reduce the chance that it will catch fire

20. The one of the following which would be considered a MINOR drawback of the XYZ Process is that it 20.____

    A. forms chars when exposed to flame
    B. makes fabrics mildew-resistant
    C. adds to the weight of fabrics
    D. is compatible with other finishing treatments

Questions 21-25.

DIRECTIONS: Questions 21 through 25 are to be answered SOLELY on the basis of the following paragraph.

In order to help prevent the spread of fire, it is necessary to understand the means by which heat is transmitted. Heat is transmitted through solids by a method called *conduction*. Materials vary greatly in their ability to transmit heat. Metals are good conductors of heat. On the other hand, wood, glass, pottery, asbestos, and many like substances are very poor conductors of heat and are termed insulators. It should be remembered, however, that there are no perfect insulators of heat. All will conduct heat to some extent; and if the heat continues long enough, it will be transmitted through the solid. The hazard of heat transmission is illustrated by the fact that a fire on one side of a metal wall could start a fire on the other side if combustibles were close to the wall.

21. Of the following, the BEST material to use for the handle of a metal pan to guard against heat is 21.____

    A. copper   B. iron   C. wood   D. steel

22. According to the above paragraph, *conduction* applies to the traveling of heat through a 22.____

    A. solid
    B. liquid
    C. slow-moving fluid
    D. gas

23. According to the information in the above paragraph, when storing combustible materials in a room with metal walls, it is BEST to 23.____

    A. keep the combustibles close together
    B. keep the combustibles away from the metal walls
    C. put the non-metals nearest the metal walls
    D. separate metal materials from non-metal materials

24. Based on the information in the above paragraph, which one of the following objects is the BEST conductor of heat? 24.____

    A. Pottery
    B. An oak desk
    C. A glass jar
    D. A silver spoon

25. Of the following, the title which BEST describes what the above paragraph is about is 25.____

    A. USES OF CONDUCTORS AND INSULATORS
    B. THE REASONS WHY FIRE SPREADS
    C. HEAT TRANSMISSION AND FIRES
    D. THE HAZARDS OF POOR CONDUCTION

KEY (CORRECT ANSWERS)

1.	C	11.	C
2.	C	12.	C
3.	D	13.	C
4.	D	14.	A
5.	C	15.	D
6.	B	16.	B
7.	D	17.	D
8.	D	18.	A
9.	C	19.	D
10.	A	20.	C

21. C
22. A
23. B
24. D
25. C

CODING

COMMENTARY

An ingenious question-type called coding, involving elements of alphabetizing, filing, name and number comparison, and evaluative judgment and application, has currently won wide acceptance in testing circles for measuring clerical aptitude and general ability, particularly on the senior (middle) grades (levels).

While the directions for this question usually vary in detail, the candidate is generally asked to consider groups of names, codes, and numbers, and, then, according to a given plan, to arrange codes in alphabetic order; to arrange these in numerical sequence; to re-arrange columns of names and numbers in correct order; to espy errors in coding; to choose the correct coding arrangement in consonance with the given directions and examples, etc.

This question-type appears to have few paramaters in respect to form, substance, or degree of difficulty.

Accordingly, acquaintance with, and practice in, the coding question is recommended for the serious candidate.

EXAMINATION SECTION
TEST 1

DIRECTIONS:

CODE TABLE

Name of Applicant	H A N G S B R U K E	
Test Code	c o m p l e x i t y	
File Number	0 1 2 3 4 5 6 7 8 9	

Assume that each of the above *capital letters* is the first letter of the Name of an Applicant, that the *small letter* directly beneath each capital letter is the Test Code for the Applicant, and that the *number* directly beneath each code letter is the File Number for the Applicant.
In each of the following questions, the test code letters and the file numbers in Columns 2 and 3 should correspond to the capital letters in Column 1. For each question, look at each column carefully and mark your answer as follows:

If there is an error only in Column 2, mark your answer A.
If there is an error only in Column 3, mark your answer B.
If there is an error in both Columns 2 and 3, mark your answer C.
If both Columns 2 and 3 are correct, mark your answer D.

The following sample question is given to help you understand the procedure.

SAMPLE QUESTION

Column 1	Column 2	Column 3
AKEHN	otyci	18902

2 (#1)

In Column 2, the final test code letter "i" should be "m." Column 3 is correctly coded to Column 1. Since there is an error only in Column 2, the answer is A

	Column 1	Column 2	Column 3
1.	NEKKU	mytti	29987
2.	KRAEB	txlye	86095
3.	ENAUK	ymoit	92178
4.	REANA	xeomo	69121
5.	EKHSE	ytcxy	97049

1.____
2.____
3.____
4.____
5.____

KEY (CORRECT ANSWERS)

1. B
2. C
3. D
4. A
5. C

TEST 2

DIRECTIONS: The employee identification codes in Column I begin and end with a capital letter and have an eight-digit number in between. In Questions 1 through 8, employee identification codes in Column I are to be arranged according to the following rules:

First: Arrange in alphabetical order according to the first letter.

Second: When two or more employee identification codes have the same first letter, arrange in alphabetical order according to the last letter.

Third: When two or more employee codes have the same first and last letters, arrange in numerical order beginning with the lowest number.

The employee identification codes in Column I are numbered 1 through 5 in the order in which they are listed. In Column II the numbers 1 through 5 are arranged in four different ways to show different arrangements of the corresponding employee identification numbers. Choose the answer in Column II in which the employee identification numbers are arranged according to the above rules.

SAMPLE QUESTION

Column I
1. E75044127B
2. B96399104A
3. B93939086A
4. B47064465H
5. B99040922A

Column II
A. 4, 1, 3, 2, 5
B. 4, 1, 2, 3, 5
C. 4, 3, 2, 5, 1
D. 3, 2, 5, 4, 1

In the sample question, the four employee identification codes starting with B should be put before the employee identification code starting with E. The employee identification codes starting with B and ending with A should be put before the employee identification codes starting with B and ending with H. The three employee identification codes starting with B and ending with A should be listed in numerical order, beginning with the lowest number. The correct way to arrange the employee identification codes, therefore, is 3, 2, 5, 4, 1 shown below.

3. B93939086A
2. B96399104A
5. B99040922A
4. B47064465H
1. E75044127B

Therefore, the answer to the sample question is D. Now answer the following questions according to the above rules.

Column I
1. 1. G42786441J
   2. H45665413J
   3. G43117690J
   4. G435466981
   5. G416799421

Column II
A. 2, 5, 4, 3, 1
B. 5, 4, 1, 3, 2
C. 4, 5, 1, 3, 2
D. 1, 3, 5, 4, 2

1.____

2 (#2)

2.
1. S44556178T
2. T43457169T
3. S53321176T
4. T53317998S
5. S67673942S

A. 1, 3, 5, 2, 4
B. 4, 3, 5, 2, 1
C. 5, 3, 1, 2, 4
D. 5, 1, 3, 4, 2

2.____

3.
1. R63394217D
2. R63931247D
3. R53931247D
4. R66874239D
4. R46799366D

A. 5, 4, 2, 3, 1
B. 1, 5, 3, 2, 4
C. 5, 3, 1, 2, 4
D. 5, 1, 2, 3, 4

3.____

4.
1. A35671968B
2. A35421794C
3. A35466987B
4. C10435779A
5. C00634779B

A. 3, 2, 1, 4, 5
B. 2, 3, 1, 5, 4
C. 1, 3, 2, 4, 5
D. 3, 1, 2, 4, 5

4.____

5.
1. I99746426Q
2. I10445311Q
3. J63749877P
4. J03421739Q
5. J00765311Q

A. 2, 1, 3, 5, 4
B. 5, 4, 2, 1, 3
C. 4, 5, 3, 2, 1
D. 2, 1, 4, 5, 3

5.____

6.
1. M33964217N
2. N33942770N
3. N06155881M
4. M00433669M
5. M79034577N

A. 4, 1, 5, 2, 3
B. 5, 1, 4, 3, 2
C. 4, 1, 5, 3, 2
D. 1, 4, 5, 2, 3

6.____

7.
1. D77643905C
2. D44106788C
3. D13976022F
4. D97655430E
5. D00439776F

A. 1, 2, 5, 3, 4
B. 5, 3, 2, 1, 4
C. 2, 1, 5, 3, 4
D. 2, 1, 4, 5, 3

7.____

8.
1. W22746920A
2. W22743720A
3. W32987655A
4. W43298765A
5. W30987433A

A. 2, 1, 3, 4, 5
B. 2, 1, 5, 3, 4
C. 1, 2, 3, 4, 5
D. 1, 2, 5, 3, 4

8.____

KEY (CORRECT ANSWERS)

1. B
2. D
3. C
4. D
5. A
6. C
7. D
8. B

TEST 3

DIRECTIONS: Each of the following equations consists of three sets of names and name codes. In each question, the two names and name codes on the same line are supposed to be exactly the same.

Look carefully at each set of names and codes and mark your answer:
- A. if there are mistakes in all three sets
- B. if there are mistakes in two of the sets
- C. if there is a mistake in only one set
- D. if there are no mistakes in any of the sets

The following sample question is given to help you understand the procedure.

Macabe, John N.	- V	53162	Macade, John N.	- V	53162
Howard, Joan S.	- J	24791	Howard, Joan S.	- J	24791
Ware, Susan B.	- A	45068	Ware, Susan B.	- A	45968

In the above sample question, the names and name codes of the first set are not exactly the same because of the spelling of the last name (Macabe - Macade). The names and name codes of the second set are exactly the same. The names and name codes of the third set are not exactly the same because the two name codes are different (A 45068 - A 45968), Since there are mistakes in only 2 of the sets, the answer to the sample question is B.

1. Powell, Michael C. - 78537 F
   Martinez, Pablo, J. - 24435 P
   MacBane, Eliot M. - 98674 E

   Powell, Michael C. - 78537 F
   Martinez, Pablo J. - 24435 P
   MacBane, Eliot M. - 98674 E

   1._____

2. Fitz-Kramer Machines Inc. - 259090
   Marvel Cleaning Service - 482657
   Donate, Carl G. - 637418

   Fitz-Kramer Machines Inc. - 259090
   Marvel Cleaning Service - 482657
   Danato, Carl G. - 687418

   2._____

3. Martin Davison Trading Corp. - 43108 T
   Cotwald Lighting Fixtures - 76065 L
   R. Crawford Plumbers - 23157 C

   Martin Davidson Trading Corp. - 43108 T
   Cotwald Lighting Fixtures - 70056 L
   R. Crawford Plumbers - 23157 G

   3._____

4. Fraiman Engineering Corp. - M4773
   Neuman, Walter B. - N7745
   Pierce, Eric M. - W6304

   Friaman Engineering Corp. -M4773
   Neumen, Walter B. - N7745
   Pierce, Eric M. - W6304

   4._____

5. Constable, Eugene - B 64837
   Derrick, Paul - H 27119
   Heller, Karen - S 49606

   Comstable, Eugene - B 64837
   Derrik, Paul - H 27119
   Heller, Karen - S 46906

   5._____

6. Hernando Delivery Service Co. - D 7456
   Barettz Electrical Supplies - N 5392
   Tanner, Abraham - M 4798

   Hernando Delivery Service Co. - D 7456
   Barettz Electrical Supplies - N 5392
   Tanner, Abraham - M 4798

   6._____

7. Kalin Associates - R 38641
   Sealey, Robert E. - P 63533
   Scalsi Office Furniture

   Kaline Associates - R 38641
   Sealey, Robert E. - P 63553
   Scalsi Office Furniture

   7._____

2 (#3)

8. Janowsky, Philip M.- 742213
    Hansen, Thomas H. - 934816
    L. Lester and Son Inc. - 294568

    Janowsky, Philip M.- 742213
    Hanson, Thomas H. - 934816
    L. Lester and Son Inc. - 294568

8.____

KEY (CORRECT ANSWERS)

1. D
2. C
3. A
4. B
5. A

6. D
7. B
8. C

---

1. A
2. C
3. B
4. B
5. D

6. 197546821 - YSUWSTPNY   6._____
   873024867 - PUZRNWPTU
   583179246 - WPZYURNXT

7. 510782463 - WYRUSNXTZ   7._____
   478192356 - XUPYSNZWT
   961728532 - STYUNPWXN

KEY (CORRECT ANSWERS)

1. A
2. C
3. B
4. B
5. D

6. C
7. B

TEST 5

DIRECTIONS: Assume that each of the capital letters is the first letter of the name of a city using EAM equipment. The number directly beneath each capital letter is the code number for the city. The small letter beneath each code number is the code letter for the number of EAM divisions in the city and the + or - symbol directly beneath each code letter is the code symbol which signifies whether or not the city uses third generation computers with the EAM equipment.

The questions that follow show City Letters in Column I, Code Numbers in Column II, Code Letters in Column III, and Code Symbols in Column IV. If correct, each City Letter in Column I should correspond by position with each of the three codes shown in the other three columns, in accordance with the coding key shown. BUT there are some errors. For each question,

If there is a total of ONE error in Columns 2, 3, and 4, mark your answer A.
If there is a total of TWO errors in Columns 2, 3, and 4, mark your answer B.
If there is a total of THREE errors in Columns 2, 3, and 4, mark your answer C.
If Columns 2, 3, and 4 are correct, mark your answer D.

SAMPLE QUESTION

I	II	III	IV
City Letter	Code Numbers	Code Letters	Code Symbols
Y J M O S	5 3 7 9 8	e b g i h	- - + + -

The errors are as follows: In Column 2, the Code Number should be "2" instead of "3" for City Letter "J," and in Column 4 the Code Symbol should be "+" instead of "-" for City Letter "Y." Since there is a total of two errors in Columns 2, 3, and 4, the answer to this sample question is B.

Now answer questions 1 through 9 according to these rules.

CODING KEY

City Letter	P	J	R	T	Y	K	M	S	O
Code Number	1	2	3	4	5	6	7	8	9
Code Letter	a	b	c	d	e	f	g	h	i
Code Symbol	+	-	+	-	+	-	+	-	+

	I City Letters	II Code Numbers	III Code Letters	IV Code Symbols	
1.	K O R M P	6 9 3 7 1	f i e g a	- - + + +	1.____
2.	O T P S Y	9 4 1 8 6	b d a h e	+ - - - +	2.____
3.	R S J T M	3 8 1 4 7	c h b e g	- - - - +	3.____
4.	P M S K J	1 7 8 6 2	a g h f b	+ + - - -	4.____
5.	M Y T J R	7 5 4 2 3	g e d f c	+ + - - +	5.____
6.	T P K Y O	4 1 6 7 9	d a f e i	- + - + -	6.____
7.	S K O R T	8 6 9 3 5	h f i c d	- - + + -	7.____
8.	J R Y P K	2 3 5 1 9	b d e a f	- + + + -	8.____
9.	R O M P Y	4 9 7 1 5	c i g a d	+ + - + +	9.____

KEY (CORRECT ANSWERS)

1. B
2. C
3. C
4. D
5. A

6. B
7. A
8. B
9. C

TEST 6

Assume that each of the capital letters is the first letter of the name of an offense, that the small letter directly beneath each capital letter is the code letter for the offense, and that the number directly beneath each code letter is the file number for the offense.

DIRECTIONS: In each of the following questions, the code letters and file numbers should correspond to the capital letters.

If there is an error only in Column 2, mark your answer A.
If there is an error only in Column 3, mark your answer B.
If there is an error in both Column 2 and Column 3, mark your answer C.
If both Columns 2 and 3 are correct, mark your answer D.

SAMPLE QUESTION

Column 1	Column 2	Column 3
BNARGHSVVU	emoxtylcci	6357905118

The code letters in Column 2 are correct but the first "5" in Column 3 should be "2." Therefore, the answer is B. Now answer the following questions according to the above rules.

CODE TABLE

Name of Offense	V	A	N	D	S	B	R	U	G	H
Code Letter	c	o	m	p	l	e	x	i	t	y
File Number	1	2	3	4	5	6	7	8	9	0

	Column 1	Column 2	Column 3	
1.	HGDSBNBSVR	ytplxmelcx	0945736517	1.____
2.	SDGUUNHVAH	lptiimycoy	5498830120	2.____
3.	BRSNAAVUDU	exlmooctpi	6753221848	3.____
4.	VSRUDNADUS	cleipmopil	1568432485	4.____
5.	NDSHVRBUAG	mplycxeiot	3450175829	5.____
6.	GHUSNVBRDA	tyilmcexpo	9085316742	6.____
7.	DBSHVURANG	pesycixomt	4650187239	7.____
8.	RHNNASBDGU	xymnolepti	7033256398	8.____

KEY (CORRECT ANSWERS)

1. C
2. D
3. A
4. C
5. B

6. D
7. A
8. C

TEST 7

DIRECTIONS: Each of the following questions contains three sets of code letters and code numbers. In each set, the code numbers should correspond with the code letters as given in the Table, but there is a coding error in some of the sets. Examine the sets in each question carefully.

Mark your answer A if there is a coding error in only *ONE* of the sets in the question.
Mark your answer B if there is a coding error in any *TWO* of the sets in the question.
Mark your answer C if there is a coding error in all *THREE* sets in the question.
Mark your answer D if there is a coding error in *NONE* of the sets in the question.

SAMPLE QUESTION

fgzduwaf - 35720843
uabsdgfw - 04262538
hhfaudgs - 99340257

In the above sample question, the first set is right because each code number matches the code letter as in the Code Table. In the second set, the corresponding number for the code letter b is wrong because it should be 1 instead of 2. In the third set, the corresponding number for the last code letter s is wrong because it should be 6 instead of 7. Since there is an error in two of the sets, the answer to the above sample question is B.

In the Code Table below, each code letter has a corresponding code number directly beneath it.

CODE TABLE

Code Letter	b	d	f	a	g	s	z	w	h	u
Code Number	1	2	3	4	5	6	7	8	9	0

1. fsbughwz - 36104987   zwubgasz - 78025467   1.____
    ghgufddb - 59583221

2. hafgdaas - 94351446   ddsfabsd - 22734162   2.____
    wgdbssgf - 85216553

3. abfbssbd - 41316712   ghzfaubs - 59734017   3.____
    sdbzfwza - 62173874

4. whfbdzag - 89412745   daaszuub - 24467001   4.____
    uzhfwssd - 07936623

5. zbadgbuh - 71425109   dzadbbsz - 27421167   5.____
    gazhwaff - 54798433

6. fbfuadsh - 31304265   gzfuwzsb - 57300671   6.____
    bashhgag - 14699535

2 (#7)

KEY (CORRECT ANSWERS)

1. B
2. C
3. B
4. B
5. D
6. C

TEST 8

DIRECTIONS: The following questions are to be answered on the basis of the following Code Table. In this table every letter has a corresponding code number to be punched. Each question contains three pairs of letters and code numbers. In each pair, the code numbers should correspond with the letters in accordance with the Code Table.

CODE TABLE

Letter	P	L	A	N	D	C	O	B	U	R
Corresponding Code Number	1	2	3	4	5	6	7	8	9	0

In some of the pairs below, an error exists in the coding. Examine the pairs in each question. Mark your answer

- A if there is a mistake in only *one* of the pairs
- B if there is a mistake in only *two* of the pairs
- C if there is a mistake in *all three* of the pairs
- D if there is a mistake in *none* of the pairs

SAMPLE QUESTION

LCBPUPAB - 26819138
ACOABOL - 3683872
NDURONUC - 46901496

In the above sample, the first pair is correct since each letter as listed has the correct corresponding code number. In the second pair, an error exists because the letter O should have the code number 7, instead of 8. In the third pair, an error exists because the letter D should have the code number 5, instead of 6. Since there are errors in two of the three pairs, your answer should be B.

1. ADCANPLC - 35635126
   PNACBUCP - 14368061
   DORURBBO - 57090877   1.____

2. LCOBLRAP - 26782931
   RLDACLRO - 02536207
   UPANUPCD - 91349156   2.____

3. LCOROPAR - 26707130
   DOPOAULL - 57173922
   BALANRUP - 83234091   3.____

4. ONCRUBAP - 74609831
   AORPDUR - 3771590
   DCLANORD - 56243705   4.____

5. PANRBUCD - 13408965
   OPDDOBRA - 71556803
   UAOCDPLR - 93765120   5.____

6. BAROLDCP - 83072561
   BURPDOLA - 89015723
   PNOCOBLA - 14767823   6.____

7. ANNCPABO - 34461387
   ACRPOUL - 3601792
   DBALDRCP - 58325061   7.____

93

2 (#8)

8. BLAPOUR - 8321790　　　NOACNPL - 4736412　　　　8. ____
　　RODACORD - 07536805

9. ADUBURCL - 3598062　　NOCOBAPR - 47578310　　　9. ____
　　PRONDALU - 10754329

10. UBADCLOR - 98356270　　NBUPPARA - 48911033　　　10. ____
　　　LONDUPRC - 27459106

KEY (CORRECT ANSWERS)

1. C
2. B
3. D
4. B
5. A

6. D
7. B
8. B
9. C
10. A

TEST 9

DIRECTIONS: Answer questions 1 through 10 ONLY on the basis of the following information.

Column I consists of serial numbers of dollar bills. Column II shows different ways of arranging the corresponding serial numbers.

The serial numbers of dollar bills in Column I begin and end with a capital letter and have an eight-digit number in between. The serial numbers in Column I are to be arranged according to the following rules:

FIRST: In alphabetical order according to the first letter.

SECOND: When two or more serial numbers have the same first letter, in alphabetical order according to the last letter.

THIRD: When two or more serial numbers have the same first *and* last letters, in numerical order, beginning with the lowest number.

The serial numbers in Column I are numbered (1) through (5) in the order in which they are listed. In Column II the numbers (1) through (5) are arranged in four different ways to show different arrangements of the corresponding serial numbers. Choose the answer in Column II in which the serial numbers are arranged according to the above rules.

SAMPLE QUESTION

COLUMN I
(1) E75044127B
(2) B96399104A
(3) B93939086A
(4) B47064465H
(5) B99040922A

COLUMN II
(A) 4, 1, 3, 2, 5
(B) 4, 1, 2, 3, 5
(C) 4, 3, 2, 5, 1
(D) 3, 2, 5, 4, 1

In the sample question, the four serial numbers starting with B should be put before the serial number starting with E. The serial numbers starting with B and ending with A should be put before the serial number starting with B and ending with H. The three serial numbers starting with B and ending with A should be listed in numerical order, beginning with the lowest number. The correct way to arrange the serial numbers, therefore, is:

(3) B93939086A
(2) B96399104A
(5) B99040922A
(4) B47064465H
(1) E75044127B

Since the order of arrangement is 3, 2, 5, 4, 1, the answer to the sample question is (D).

COLUMN I
1. (1) P44343314Y
   (2) P44141341S
   (3) P44141431L
   (4) P41143413W
   (5) P44313433H
2. (1) D89077275M
   (2) D98073724N
   (3) D90877274N
   (4) D98877275M
   (5) D98873725N

COLUMN II
1.
A. 2, 3, 1, 4, 5
B. 1, 5, 3, 2, 4
C. 4, 2, 3, 5, 1
D. 5, 3, 2, 4, 1

2.
A. 3, 2, 5, 4, 1
B. 1, 4, 3, 2, 5
C. 4, 1, 5, 2, 3
D. 1, 3, 2, 5, 4

95

3.	(1)	H32548137E		A.	2,	4,	5,	1,	3
	(2)	H35243178A		B.	1,	5,	2,	3,	4
	(3)	H35284378F		C.	1,	5,	2,	4,	3
	(4)	H35288337A		D.	2,	1,	5,	3,	4
	(5)	H32883173B							
4.	(1)	K24165039H		A.	4,	2,	5,	3,	1
	(2)	F24106599A		B.	2,	3,	4,	1,	5
	(3)	L21406639G		C.	4,	2,	5,	1,	3
	(4)	C24156093A		D.	1,	3,	4,	5,	2
	(5)	K24165593D							
5.	(1)	H79110642E		A.	2,	1,	3,	5,	4
	(2)	H79101928E		B.	2,	1,	4,	5,	3
	(3)	A79111567F		C.	3,	5,	2,	1,	4
	(4)	H79111796E		D.	4,	3,	5,	1,	2
	(5)	A79111618F							
6.	(1)	P16388385W		A.	3,	4,	5,	2,	1
	(2)	R16388335V		B.	2,	3,	4,	5,	1
	(3)	P16383835W		C.	2,	4,	3,	1,	5
	(4)	R18386865V		D.	3,	1,	5,	2,	4
	(5)	P18686865W							
7.	(1)	B42271749G		A.	4,	1,	5,	2,	3
	(2)	B42271779G		B.	4,	1,	2,	5,	3
	(3)	E43217779G		C.	1,	2,	4,	5,	3
	(4)	B42874119C		D.	5,	3,	1,	2,	4
	(5)	E42817749G							
8.	(1)	M57906455S		A.	4,	1,	5,	3,	2
	(2)	N87077758S		B.	3,	4,	1,	5,	2
	(3)	N87707757B		C.	4,	1,	5,	2,	3
	(4)	M57877759B		D.	1,	5,	3,	2,	4
	(5)	M57906555S							
9.	(1)	C69336894Y		A.	2,	5,	3,	1,	4
	(2)	C69336684V		B.	3,	2,	5,	1,	4
	(3)	C69366887W		C.	3,	1,	4,	5,	2
	(4)	C69366994Y		D.	2,	5,	1,	3,	4
	(5)	C69336865V							
10.	(1)	A56247181D		A.	1,	5,	3,	2,	4
	(2)	A56272128P		B.	3,	1,	5,	2,	4
	(3)	H56247128D		C.	3,	2,	1,	5,	4
	(4)	H56272288P		D.	1,	5,	2,	3,	4
	(5)	A56247188D							

KEY (CORRECT ANSWERS)

1. D 6. D
2. B 7. B
3. A 8. A
4. C 9. A
5. C 10. D

TEST 10

DIRECTIONS: Answer the following questions on the basis of the instructions, the code, and the sample questions given below. Assume that an officer at a certain location is equipped with a two-way radio to keep him in constant touch with his security headquarters. Radio messages and replies are given in code form, as follows:

CODE TABLE

Radio Code for Situation	J	P	M	F	B
Radio Code for Action to be Taken	o	r	a	z	q
Radio Response for Action Being Taken	1	2	3	4	5

Assume that each of the above capital letters is the radio code for a particular type of situation, that the small letter below each capital letter is the radio code for the action an officer is directed to take, and that the number directly below each small letter is the radio response an officer should make to indicate what action was actually taken.

In each of the following questions, the code letter for the action directed (Column 2) and the code number for the action taken (Column 3) should correspond to the capital letters in Column 1.

INSTRUCTIONS: If only Column 2 is different from Column 1, mark your answer I.
If only Column 3 is different from Column 1, mark your answer II.
If both Column 2 and Column 3 are different from Column I, mark your answer III.
If both Columns 2 and 3 are the same as Column 1, mark your answer IV.

SAMPLE QUESTION

Column 1	Column 2	Column 3
JPFMB	orzaq	12453

The CORRECT answer is: A. I B. II C. III D. IV

The code letters in Column 2 are correct, but the numbers "53" in Column 3 should be "35." Therefore, the answer is B. Now answe the following questions according to the above rules.

	Column 1	Column 2	Column 3
1.	PBFJM	rqzoa	25413
2.	MPFBJ	zrqao	32541
3.	JBFPM	oqzra	15432
4.	BJPMF	qaroz	51234
5.	PJFMB	rozaq	21435
6.	FJBMP	zoqra	41532

KEY (CORRECT ANSWERS)

1. D
2. C
3. B
4. A
5. D
6. A

CLERICAL ABILITIES TEST
EXAMINATION SECTION
TEST 1

DIRECTIONS: Each question or incomplete statement is followed by several suggested answers or completions. Select the one that BEST answers the question or completes the statement. *PRINT THE LETTER OF THE CORRECT ANSWER IN THE SPACE AT THE RIGHT.*

Questions 1-10.

DIRECTIONS: Questions 1 through 10 consist of lines of names, dates, and numbers. For each question, you are to choose the option (A, B, C, or D) in Column II which EXACTLY matches the information in Column I. *PRINT THE LETTER OF THE CORRECT ANSWER IN THE SPACE AT THE RIGHT.*

SAMPLE QUESTION

Column I
Schneider 11/16/75 581932

Column II
A. Schneider 11/16/75 518932
B. Schneider 11/16/75 581932
C. Schnieder 11/16/75 581932
D. Shnieder   11/16/75 518932

The correct answer is B. Only Option B shows the name, date, and number exactly as they are in Column I. Option A has a mistake in the number. Option C has a mistake in the name. Option D has a mistake in the name and in the number. Now answer Questions 1 through 10 in the same manner.

Column I
1. Johnston 12/26/74 659251

   Column II
   A. Johnson   12/23/74 659251
   B. Johston   12/26/74 659251
   C. Johnston 12/26/74 695251
   D. Johnston 12/26/74 659251

   1.____

2. Allison 1/26/75 9939256

   A. Allison 1/26/75 9939256
   B. Alisson 1/26/75 9939256
   C. Allison 1/26/76 9399256
   D. Allison 1/26/75 9993356

   2.____

3. Farrell 2/12/75 361251

   A. Farell   2/21/75 361251
   B. Farrell 2/12/75 361251
   C. Farrell 2/21/75 361251
   D. Farrell 2/12/75 361151

   3.____

4. Guerrero 4/28/72 105689
    A. Guerrero 4/28/72 105689
    B. Guerrero 4/28/72 105986
    C. Guerrero 4/28/72 105869
    D. Guerrero 4/28/72 105689

    4._____

5. McDonnell 6/05/73 478215
    A. McDonnell 6/15/73 478215
    B. McDonnell 6/05/73 478215
    C. McDonnell 6/05/73 472815
    D. MacDonell 6/05/73 478215

    5._____

6. Shepard 3/31/71 075421
    A. Sheperd 3/31/71 075421
    B. Shepard 3/13/71 075421
    C. Shepard 3/31/71 075421
    D. Shepard 3/13/71 075241

    6._____

7. Russell 4/01/69 031429
    A. Russell 4/01/69 031429
    B. Russell 4/10/69 034129
    C. Russell 4/10/69 031429
    D. Russell 4/01/69 034129

    7._____

8. Phillips 10/16/68 961042
    A. Philipps 10/16/68 961042
    B. Phillips 10/16/68 960142
    C. Phillips 10/16/68 961042
    D. Philipps 10/16/68 916042

    8._____

9. Campbell 11/21/72 624856
    A. Campbell 11/21/72 624856
    B. Campbell 11/21/72 624586
    C. Campbell 11/21/72 624686
    D. Campbel 11/21/72 624856

    9._____

10. Patterson 9/18/71 76199176
    A. Patterson 9/18/72 76191976
    B. Patterson 9/18/71 76199176
    C. Patterson 9/18/72 76199176
    D. Patterson 9/18/71 76919176

    10._____

Questions 11-15.

DIRECTIONS: Questions 11 through 15 consist of groups of numbers and letters which you are to compare. For each question, you are to choose the option (A, B,C, or D) in Column I which EXACTLY matches the group of numbers and letters given in Column I.

SAMPLE QUESTION

Column I
B92466

Column II
A. B92644
B. B94266
C. A92466
D. B92466

The correct answer is D. Only Option D in Column II shows the group of numbers and letters EXACTLY as it appears in Column I. Now answer Questions 11 through 15 in the same manner.

<u>Column I</u>

11. 925AC5

12. Y006925

13. J236956

14. AB6952

15. X259361

<u>Column II</u>

11.
A. 952CA5
B. 925AC5
C. 952AC5
D. 925CA6

12.
A. Y060925
B. Y006295
C. Y006529
D. Y006925

13.
A. J236956
B. J326965
C. J239656
D. J932656

14.
A. AB6952
B. AB9625
C. AB9652
D. AB6925

15.
A. X529361
B. X259631
C. X523961
D. X259361

11.____

12.____

13.____

14.____

15.____

Questions 16-25.

DIRECTIONS: Each of questions 16 through 25 consists of three lines of code letters and three lines of numbers. The numbers on each line should correspond with the code letters on the same line in accordance with the table below.

Code Letter	S	V	W	A	Q	M	X	E	G	K
Corresponding Number	0	1	2	3	4	5	5	7	8	9

On some of the lines, an error exists in the coding. Compare the letters and numbers in each question carefully. If you find an error or errors on:
  only one of the lines in the question, mark your answer A;
  any two lines in the question, mark your answer B;
  all three lines in the question, mark your answer C;
  none of the lines in the question, mark your answer D.

4 (#1)

SAMPLE QUESTION

WQGKSXG	2489068
XEKVQMA	6591453
KMAESXV	9527061

In the above sample, the first line is correct since each code letter listed has the correct corresponding number. On the second line, an error exists because code letter E should have the number 7 instead of the number 5. On the third line, an error exists because the code letter A should have the number 3 instead of the number 2. Since there are errors in two of the three lines, the correct answer is B. Now answer Questions 16 through 25 in the same manner.

16. SWQEKGA   0247983   16.____
     KEAVSXM   9731065
     SSAXGKQ   0036894

17. QAMKMVS   4259510   17.____
     MGGEASX   5897306
     KSWMKWS   9125920

18. WKXQWVE   2964217   18.____
     QKXXQVA   4966413
     AWMXGVS   3253810

19. GMMKASE   8559307   19.____
     AWVSKSW   3210902
     QAVSVGK   4310189

20. XGKQSMK   6894049   20.____
     QSVKEAS   4019730
     GSMXKMV   8057951

21. AEKMWSG   3195208   21.____
     MKQSVQK   5940149
     XGQAEVW   6843712

22. XGMKAVS   6858310   22.____
     SKMAWEQ   0953174
     GVMEQSA   8167403

23. VQSKAVE   1489317   23.____
     WQGKAEM   2489375
     MEGKAWQ   5689324

24. XMQVSKG   6541098   24.____
     QMEKEWS   4579720
     KMEVGKG   9571983

25. GKVAMEW   88912572   25._____
     AXMVKAE   3651937
     KWAGMAV   9238531

Questions 26-35.

DIRECTIONS: Each of Questions 26 through 35 consists of a column of figures. For each question, add the column of figures and choose the correct answer from the four choices given.

26. 5,665.43   26._____
     2,356.69
     6,447.24
     7,239.65

     A. 20,698.01   B. 21,709.01
     C. 21,718.01   D. 22,609.01

27. 817,209.55   27._____
     264,354.29
      82,368.76
     849,964.89

     A. 1,893.977.49   B. 1,989,988.39
     C. 2,009,077.39   D. 2,013,897.49

28. 156,366.89   28._____
     249,973.23
     823,229.49
      56,869.45

     A. 1,286,439.06   B. 1,287,521.06
     C. 1,297,539.06   D. 1,296,421.06

29.   23,422.15   29._____
     149,696.24
     238,377.53
      86,289.79
     505,533.63

     A. 989,229.34   B. 999,879.34
     C. 1,003,330.34   D. 1,023,329.34

6 (#1)

30. 2,468,926.70
    656,842.28
     49,723.15
    832,369.59

    A. 3,218,062.72   B. 3,808,092.72
    C. 4,007,861.72   D. 4,818,192.72

30.____

31.   524,201.52
   7,775,678.51
   8,345,299.63
  40,628,898.08
  31,374,670.07

    A. 88,646,647.81   B. 88,646,747.91
    C. 88,648,647.91   D. 88,648,747.81

31.____

32. 6,824,829.40
    682,482.94
  5,542,015.27
    775,678.51
  7,732,507.25

    A. 21,557,513.37   B. 21,567,513.37
    C. 22,567,503.37   D. 22,567,513.37

32.____

33. 22,109,405.58
   6,097,093.43
   5,050,073.99
   8,118,050.05
   4,313,980.82

    A. 45,688,593.87   B. 45,688,603.87
    C. 45,689,593.87   D. 45,689,603.87

33.____

34. 79,324,114.19
   99,848,129.74
   43,331,653.31
   41,610,207.14

    A. 264,114,104.38   B. 264,114,114.38
    C. 265,114,114.38   D. 265,214,104.38

34.____

35. 33,729,653.94
    5,959,342.58
    26,052,715.47
    4,452,669.52
    7,079,953.59

   A. 76,374,334.10 B. 76,375,334.10
   C. 77,274,335.10 D. 77,275,335.10

35.____

Questions 36-40.

DIRECTIONS: Each of Questions 36 through 40 consists of a single number in Column I and four options in Column II. For each question, you are to choose the option (A, B, C, or D) in Column II which EXACTLY matches the number in Column I.

SAMPLE QUESTION

Column I
5965121

Column II
A. 5956121
B. 5965121
C. 5966121
D. 5965211

The correct answer is B. Only Option B shows the number EXACTLY as it appears in Column I. Now answer Questions 36 through 40 in the same manner.

Column I
36. 9643242

Column II
A. 9643242
B. 9462342
C. 9642442
D. 9463242

36.____

37. 3572477

A. 3752477
B. 3725477
C. 3572477
D. 3574277

37.____

38. 5276101

A. 5267101
B. 5726011
C. 5271601
D. 5276101

38.____

39. 4469329

A. 4496329
B. 4469329
C. 4496239
D. 4469239

39.____

40. 2326308   A. 2236308   40. ____
                      B. 2233608
                      C. 2326308
                      D. 2323608

_____

KEY (CORRECT ANSWERS)

1.	D	11.	B	21.	A	31.	D
2.	A	12.	D	22.	C	32.	A
3.	B	13.	A	23.	B	33.	B
4.	D	14.	A	24.	D	34.	A
5.	B	15.	D	25.	A	35.	C
6.	C	16.	D	26.	B	36.	A
7.	A	17.	C	27.	D	37.	C
8.	C	18.	A	28.	A	38.	D
9.	A	19.	D	29.	C	39.	B
10.	B	20.	B	30.	C	40.	C

TEST 2

DIRECTIONS: Each question or incomplete statement is followed by several suggested answers or completions. Select the one that BEST answers the question or completes the statement. *PRINT THE LETTER OF THE CORRECT ANSWER IN THE SPACE AT THE RIGHT.*

Questions 1-5.

DIRECTIONS: Each of Questions 1 through 5 consists of a name and a dollar amount. In each question, the name and dollar amount in Column II should be an EXACT copy of the name and dollar amount in Column I. If there is:
  a mistake only in the name, mark your answer A;
  a mistake only in the dollar amount, mark your answer B;
  a mistake in both the name and the dollar amount, mark your answer C;
  no mistake in either the name or the dollar amount, mark your answer D.

SAMPLE QUESTION

Column I
George Peterson
$125.50

Column II
George Petersson
$125.50

Compare the name and dollar amount in Column II with the name and dollar amount in Column I. The name *Petersson* in Column II is spelled *Peterson* in Column I. The amount is the same in both columns. Since there is a mistake only in the name, the answer to the sample question is A. Now answer Questions 1 through 5 in the same manner.

	Column I	Column II	
1.	Susanne Shultz $3440	Susanne Schultz $3440	1.____
2.	Anibal P. Contrucci $2121.61	Anibel P. Contrucci $2112.61	2.____
3.	Eugenio Mendoza $12.45	Eugenio Mendozza $12.45	3.____
4.	Maurice Gluckstadt $4297	Maurice Gluckstadt $4297	4.____
5.	John Pampellonne $4656.94	John Pammpellonne $4566.94	5.____

Questions 6-11.

DIRECTIONS: Each of Questions 6 through 11 consist of a set of names and addresses, which you are to compare. In each question, the name and addresses in Column II should be an EXACT copy of the name and address in Column I. If there is:
- a mistake only in the name, mark your answer A;
- a mistake only in the address, mark your answer B;
- a mistake in both the name and address, mark your answer C;
- no mistake in either the name or address, mark your answer D.

SAMPLE QUESTION

Column I	Column II
Michael Filbert	Michael Filbert
456 Reade Street	645 Reade Street
New York, N.Y. 10013	New York, N.Y. 10013

Since there is a mistake only in the address (the street number should be 456 instead of 645), the answer to the sample question is B. Now answer Questions 6 through 11 in the same manner.

#	Column I	Column II
6.	Hilda Goettelmann 55 Lenox Rd. Brooklyn, N.Y. 11226	Hilda Goettelman 55 Lenox Ave. Brooklyn, N.Y. 11226
7.	Arthur Sherman 2522 Batchelder St. Brooklyn, N.Y. 11235	Arthur Sharman 2522 Batcheder St. Brooklyn, N.Y. 11253
8.	Ralph Barnett 300 West 28 Street New York, New York 10001	Ralph Barnett 300 West 28 Street New York, New York 10001
9.	George Goodwin 135 Palmer Avenue Staten Island, New York 10302	George Godwin 135 Palmer Avenue Staten Island, New York 10302
10.	Alonso Ramirez 232 West 79 Street New York, N.Y. 10024	Alonso Ramirez 223 West 79 Street New York, N.Y. 10024
11.	Cynthia Graham 149-34 83 Street Howard Beach, N.Y. 11414	Cynthia Graham 149-35 83 Street Howard Beach, N.Y. 11414

Questions 12-20.

DIRECTIONS: Questions 12 through 20 are problems in subtraction. For each question do the subtraction and select your answer from the four choices given.

12. 232,921.85
     -179,587.68

   A. 52,433.17   B. 52,434.17
   C. 53,334.17   D. 53,343,17

12.____

13. 5,531,876.29
     -3,897,158.36

   A. 1,634,717.93   B. 1,644,718.93
   C. 1,734,717.93   D. 1,7234,718.93

13.____

14. 1,482,658.22
     -937,925.76

   A. 544,633.46   B. 544,732.46
   C. 545,632.46   D. 545,732.46

14.____

15. 937,828.17
     -259,673.88

   A. 678,154.29   B. 679,154.29
   C. 688,155.39   D. 699,155.39

15.____

16. 760,412.38
     -263,465.95

   A. 496,046.43   B. 496,946.43
   C. 496,956.43   D. 497,046.43

16.____

17. 3,203,902.26
     -2,933,087.96

   A. 260,814.30   B. 269,824.30
   C. 270,814.30   D. 270,824.30

17.____

18. 1,023,468.71
     -934,678.88

   A. 88,780.83   B. 88,789.83
   C. 88,880.83   D. 88,889.83

18.____

19. 831,549.47
    -772,814.78

    A. 58,734.69   B. 58,834.69
    C. 59,735.69   D. 59,834.69

20. 6,306,181.74
    -3,617,376.99

    A. 2,687,904.99   B. 2,688,904.99
    C. 2,689,804.99   D. 2,799,905.99

Questions 21-30.

DIRECTIONS: Each of Questions 21 through 30 consists of three lines of code letters and three lines of numbers. The numbers on each line should correspond with the code letters on the same line in accordance with the table below.

Code Letter	J	U	B	T	Y	D	K	R	L	P
Corresponding Number	0	1	2	3	4	5	5	7	8	9

On some of the lines, an error exists in the coding. Compare the letters and numbers in each question carefully. If you find an error or errors on:
  only *one* of the lines in the question, mark your answer A;
  any *two* lines in the question, mark your answer B;
  all *three* lines in the question, mark your answer C;
  none of the lines in the question, mark your answer D.

SAMPLE QUESTION

    BJRPYUR   2079417
    DTBPYKJ   5328460
    YKLDBLT   4685283

In the above sample, the first line is correct since each code letter listed has the correct corresponding number. On the second line, an error exists because code letter P should have the number 9 instead of the number 8. The third line is correct since each code letter listed has the correct corresponding number. Since there is an error in *one* of the three lines, the correct answer is A. Now answer Questions 21 through 30 in the same manner.

21. BYPDTJL   2495308
    PLRDTJU   9815301
    DTJRYLK   5207486

22. RPBYRJK   7934706
    PKTYLBU   9624821
    KDLPJYR   6489047

23.	TPYBUJR	3942107	23.____
	BYRKPTU	2476931	
	DUKPYDL	5169458	
24.	KBYDLPL	6345898	24.____
	BLRKBRU	2876261	
	JTULDYB	0318542	
25.	LDPYDKR	8594567	25.____
	BDKDRJL	2565708	
	BDRPLUJ	2679810	
26.	PLRLBPU	9858291	26.____
	LPYKRDJ	88936750	
	TDKPDTR	3569527	
27.	RKURPBY	7617924	27.____
	RYUKPTJ	7426930	
	RTKPTJD	7369305	
28.	DYKPBJT	5469203	28.____
	KLPJBTL	6890238	
	TKPLBJP	3698209	
29.	BTPRJYL	2397148	29.____
	LDKUTYR	8561347	
	YDBLRPJ	4528190	
30.	ULPBKYT	1892643	30.____
	KPDTRBJ	6953720	
	YLKJPTB	4860932	

KEY (CORRECT ANSWERS)

1.	A	11.	D	21.	B
2.	C	12.	C	22.	C
3.	A	13.	A	23.	D
4.	D	14.	B	24.	B
5.	C	15.	A	25.	A
6.	C	16.	B	26.	C
7.	C	17.	C	27.	A
8.	D	18.	B	28.	D
9.	A	19.	A	29.	B
10.	B	20.	B	30.	D

NAME AND NUMBER CHECKING
EXAMINATION SECTION
TEST 1

DIRECTIONS: Questions 1 through 17 consist of sets of names and addresses. In each question, the name and address in Column II should be an exact copy of the name and address in Column I.
If there is:
a mistake only in the name, mark your answer A;
a mistake only in the address, mark your answer B;
a mistake in both name and address, mark your answer C;
No mistake in either name or address, mark your answer D.

Sample Question

Column I
Christina Magnusson
288 Greene Street
New York, N.Y. 10003

Column II
Christina Magnusson
288 Greene Street
New York, N.Y. 10013

Since there is a mistake only in the address (the zip code should be 10003 instead of 10013), the answer to the sample question is B.

COLUMN I

1. Ms. Joan Kelly
   313 Franklin Avenue
   Brooklyn, N.Y. 11202

2. Mrs. Eileen Engel
   47-24 86 Road
   Queens, N.Y. 11122

3. Marcia Michaels
   213 E. 81 St.
   New York, N.Y. 10012

4. Rev. Edward J. Smyth
   1401 Brandeis Street
   San Francisco, Calif. 96201

5. Alicia Rodriguez
   24-68 82 St.
   Elmhurst, N.Y. 11122

COLUMN II

Ms. Joan Kielly
318 Franklin Ave.
Brooklyn, N.Y. 11202

Mrs. Ellen Engel
47-24 86 Road
Queens, New York 11122

Marcia Michaels
213 E. 81 St.
New York, N.Y. 10012

Rev. Edward J. Smyth
1401 Brandies Street
San Francisco, Calif. 96201

Alicia Rodriguez
2468 81 St.
Elmhurst, N.Y. 11122

1.____

2.____

3.____

4.____

5.____

2 (#1)

COLUMN I	COLUMN II	
6. Ernest Eisemann 21 Columbia St. New York, N.Y. 10007	Ernest Eisermann 21 Columbia St. New York, N.Y. 10007	6.____
7. Mr. & Mrs. George Petersson 87-11 91st Avenue Woodhaven, N.Y. 11421	Mr. & Mrs. George Peterson 87-11 91st Avenue Woodhaven, N.Y. 11421	7.____
8. Mr. Ivan Klebnikov 1848 Newkirk Avenue Brooklyn, N.Y. 11226	Mr. Ivan Klebikov 1848 Newkirk Avenue Brooklyn, N.Y. 11622	8.____
9. Mr. Samuel Rothfleisch 71 Pine Street New York, N.Y. 10005	Samuel Rothfleisch 71 Pine Street New York, N.Y. 100005	9.____
10. Mrs. Isabel Tonnessen 198 East 185th Street Bronx, N.Y. 10458	Mrs. Isabel Tonnessen 189 East 185th Street Bronx, N.Y. 10348	10.____
11. Esteban Perez 173 Eighth Street Staten Island, N.Y. 10306	Estaban Perez 173 Eighth Street Staten Island, N.Y. 10306	11.____
12. Esta Wong 141 West 68 St. New York, N.Y. 10023	Esta Wang 141 West 68 St. New York, N.Y. 10023	12.____
13. Dr. Alberto Grosso 3475 12th Avenue Brooklyn, N.Y. 11218	Dr. Alberto Grosso 3475 12th Avenue Brooklyn, N.Y. 11218	13.____
14. Mrs. Ruth Bortias 482 Theresa Ct. Far Rockaway, N.Y. 11691	Ms. Ruth Bortlas 482 Theresa Ct. Far Rockaway, N.Y. 11169	14.____
15. Mr. & Mrs. Howard Fox 2301 Sedgwick Ave. Bronx, N.Y. 10468	Mr. & Mrs. Howard Fox 231 Sedgwick Ave. Bronx, N.Y. 10468	15.____
16. Miss Marjorie Black 223 East 23 Street New York, N.Y. 10010	Miss Margorie Black 223 East 23 Street New York, N.Y. 10010	16.____

3 (#1)

COLUMN I	COLUMN II	
17. Michelle Herman 806 Valley Rd. Old Tappan, N.J. 07675	Michelle Hermann 806 Valley Dr. Old Tappan, N.J. 07675	17.____

KEY (CORRECT ANSWERS)

1.	C	7.	A	13.	D
2.	A	8.	C	14.	C
3.	D	9.	D	15.	B
4.	B	10.	B	16.	A
5.	B	11.	A	17.	C
6.	A	12.	D		

TEST 2

DIRECTIONS: Questions 1 through 15 are to be answered SOLELY on the instructions given below. *PRINT THE LETTER OF THE CORRECT ANSWER IN THE SPACE AT THE RIGHT.*

INSTRUCTIONS

In each of the following questions, the 3-line name and address in Column I is the master-list entry, and the 3-line entry in Column II is the information to be checked against the master list. If there is one line that does not match, mark your answer A; if there are two lines that do not match, mark your answer B; if all three lines do not match, mark your answer C; if the lines all match exactly, mark your answer D.

Sample Question

Column I
Mark L. Field
11-09 Price Park Blvd.
Bronx, N.Y. 11402

Column II
Mark L. Field
11-99 Prince Park Way
Bronx, N.Y. 11401

The first lines in each column match exactly. The second lines do not match since 11-09 does not match 11-<u>99</u>; and Blvd. does not match <u>Way</u>. The third lines do not match either since 1140<u>2</u> does not match 1140<u>1</u>. Therefore, there are two lines that do not match, and the CORRECT answer is B.

	COLUMN I	COLUMN II	
1.	Jerome A. Jackson 1243 14th Avenue New York, N.Y. 10023	Jerome A. Johnson 1234 14th Avenue New York, N.Y. 10023	1.____
2.	Sophie Strachtheim 33-28 Connecticut Ave. Far Rockaway, N.Y. 11697	Sophie Strachtheim 33-28 Connecticut Ave. Far Rockaway, N.Y. 11697	2.____
3.	Elisabeth N.T. Gorrell 256 Exchange St. New York, N.Y. 10013	Elizabeth N.T. Gorrell 256 Exchange St. New York, N.Y. 10013	3.____
4.	Maria J. Gonzalez 7516 E. Sheepshead Rd. Brooklyn, N.Y. 11240	Maria J. Gonzalez 7516 N. Shepshead Rd. Brooklyn, N.Y. 11240	4.____
5.	Leslie B. Brautenweiler 21 57A Seiler Terr. Flushing, N.Y. 11367	Leslie B. Brautenwieler 21-75A Seiler Terr. Flushing, N.J. 11367	5.____

2 (#2)

COLUMN I	COLUMN II	
6. Rigoberto J. Peredes 157 Twin Towers, #18F Tottenville, S. I., N.Y,	Rigoberto J. Peredes 157 Twin Towers, #18F Tottenville, S.I., N.Y.	6.____
7. Pietro F. Albino P.O. Box 7548 Floral Park, N.Y. 11005	Pietro F. Albina P.O. Box 7458 Floral Park, N.Y. 11005	7.____
8. Joanne Zimmerman Bldg. SW, Room 314 532-4601	Joanne Zimmermann Bldg. SW, Room 314 532-4601	8.____
9. Carlyle Whetstone Payroll Div. –A, Room 212A 262-5000, ext. 471	Carlyle Whetstone Payroll Div. –A, Room 212A 262-5000, ext. 417	9.____
10. Kenneth Chiang Legal Council, Room 9745 (201) 416-9100, ext. 17	Kenneth Chiang Legal Counsel, Room 9745 (201) 416-9100, Ext. 17	10.____
11. Ethel Koenig Personnel Services Division, Room 433; 635-7572	Ethel Hoenig Personal Services Division, Room 433; 635-7527	11.____
12. Joyce Ehrhardt Office of the Administrator, Room W56; 387-8706	Joyce Ehrhart Office of the Administrator, Room W56; 387-7806	12.____
13. Ruth Lang EAM Bldg., Room C101 625-2000, ext. 765	Ruth Lang EAM Bldg., Room C110 625-2000, ext. 765	13.____
14. Anne Marie Ionozzi Investigations, Room 827 576-4000, ext. 832	Anna Marie Ionozzi Investigation, Room 827 566-4000, ext. 832	14.____
15. Willard Jameson Fm C Bldg., Room 687 454-3010	Willard Jamieson Fm C Bldg., Room 687 454-3010	15.____

KEY (CORRECT ANSWERS)

1.	B	6.	D	11.	C
2.	D	7.	B	12.	B
3.	A	8.	D	13.	A
4.	A	9.	B	14.	C
5.	C	10.	A	15.	A

TEST 3

DIRECTIONS: Questions 1 through 10 are to be answered on the basis of the following instructions. *PRINT THE LETTER OF THE CORRECT ANSWER IN THE SPACE AT THE RIGHT.*

INSTRUCTIONS
For each such set of names, addresses, and numbers listed in Columns I and II, select your answer from the following options:
- The names in Columns I and II are different,
- The addresses in Columns I and II are different,
- The numbers in Columns I and II are different,
- The names, addresses, and numbers in Columns I and II are identical.

	COLUMN I	COLUMN II	
1.	Francis Jones 62 Stately Avenue 96-12446	Francis Jones 62 Stately Avenue 96-21446	1.____
2.	Julio Montez 19 Ponderosa Road 56-73161	Julio Montez 19 Ponderosa Road 56-71361	2.____
3.	Mary Mitchell 2314 Melbourne Drive 68-92172	Mary Mitchell 2314 Melbourne Drive 68-92172	3.____
4.	Harry Patterson 25 Dunne Street 14-33430	Harry Patterson 25 Dunne Street 14-34330	4.____
5.	Patrick Murphy 171 West Hosmer Street 93-81214	Patrick Murphy 171 West Hosmer Street 93-18214	5.____
6.	August Schultz 816 St. Clair Avenue 53-40149	August Schultz 816 St. Claire Avenue 53-40149	6.____
7.	George Taft 72 Runnymede Street 47-04033	George Taft 72 Runnymede Street 47-04023	7.____
8.	Angus Henderson 1418 Madison Street 81-76375	Angus Henderson 1318 Madison Street 81-76375	8.____

COLUMN I	COLUMN II	
9. Carolyn Mazur 12 Riverview Road 38-99615	Carolyn Mazur 12 Rivervane Road 38-99615	9.____
10. Adele Russell 1725 Lansing Lane 72-91962	Adela Russell 1725 Lansing Lane 72-91962	10.____

KEY (CORRECT ANSWERS)

1. C   6. B
2. C   7. C
3. D   8. D
4. C   9. B
5. C   10. A

TEST 4

DIRECTIONS: Questions 1 through 20 test how good you are at catching mistakes in typing or printing. In each question, the name and address in Column II should be an exact copy of the name and address in Column I. Mark your answer
A. If there is no mistake in either name or address;
B. If there is a mistake in both name and address;
C. If there is a mistake only in the name;
D. If there is a mistake only in the address.
PRINT THE LETTER OF THE CORRECT ANSWER IN THE SPACE AT THE RIGHT.

COLUMN I | COLUMN II

1. Milos Yanocek
33-60 14 Street
Long Island City, N.Y. 11011

   Milos Yanocek
33-60 14 Street
Long Island City, N.Y. 11001

   1.____

2. Alphonse Sabattelo
24 Minnetta Lane
New York, N.Y. 10006

   Alphonse Sabbattelo
24 Minetta Lane
New York, N.Y. 10006

   2.____

3. Helen Steam
5 Metropolitan Oval
Bronx, N.Y. 10462

   Helene Stearn
5 Metropolitan Oval
Bronx, N.Y. 10462

   3.____

4. Jacob Weisman
231 Francis Lewis Boulevard
Forest Hills, N.Y. 11325

   Jacob Weisman
231 Francis Lewis Boulevard
Forest Hills, N.Y. 11325

   4.____

5. Riccardo Fuente
134 West 83 Street
New York, N.Y. 10024

   Riccardo Fuentes
134 West 88 Street
New York, N.Y. 10024

   5.____

6. Dennis Lauber
52 Avenue D
Brooklyn, N.Y. 11216

   Dennis Lauder
52 Avenue D
Brooklyn, N.Y. 11216

   6.____

7. Paul Cutter
195 Galloway Avenue
Staten Island, N.Y. 10356

   Paul Cutter
175 Galloway Avenue
Staten Island, N.Y. 10365

   7.____

8. Sean Donnelly
45-58 41 Avenue
Woodside, N.Y. 11168

   Sean Donnelly
45-58 41 Avenue
Woodside, N.Y. 11168

   8.____

9. Clyde Willot
1483 Rockaway Avenue
Brooklyn, N.Y. 11238

   Clyde Willat
1483 Rockaway Avenue
Brooklyn, N.Y. 11238

   9.____

COLUMN I

COLUMN II

10. Michael Stanakis
419 Sheriden Avenue
Staten Island, N.Y. 10363

    Michael Stanakis
419 Sheraden Avenue
Staten Island, N.Y. 10363   10.____

11. Joseph DiSilva
63-84 Saunders Road
Rego Park, N.Y. 11431

    Joseph Disilva
64-83 Saunders Road
Rego Park, N.Y. 11431   11.____

12. Linda Polansky
2224 Fendon Avenue
Bronx, N.Y. 20464

    Linda Polansky
2255 Fenton Avenue
Bronx, N.Y. 10464   12.____

13. Alfred Klein
260 Hillside Terrace
Staten Island, N.Y. 15545

    Alfred Klein
260 Hillside Terrace
Staten Island, N.Y. 15545   13.____

14. William McDonnell
504 E. 55 Street
New York, N.Y. 10103

    William McConnell
504 E. 55 Street
New York, N.Y. 10108   14.____

15. Angela Cipolla
41-11 Parson Avenue
Flushing, N.Y. 11446

    Angela Cipola
41-11 Parsons Avenue
Flushing, N.Y. 11446   15.____

16. Julie Sheridan
1212 Ocean Avenue
Brooklyn, N.Y. 11237

    Julia Sheridan
1212 Ocean Avenue
Brooklyn, N.Y. 11237   16.____

17. Arturo Rodriguez
2156 Cruger Avenue
Bronx, N.Y. 10446

    Arturo Rodrigues
2156 Cruger Avenue
Bronx, N.Y. 10446   17.____

18. Helen McCabe
2044 East 19 Street
Brooklyn, N.Y. 11204

    Helen McCabe
2040 East 19 Street
Brooklyn, N.Y. 11204   18.____

19. Charles Martin
526 West 160 Street
New York, N.Y. 10022

    Charles Martin
526 West 160 Street
New York, N.Y. 10022   19.____

20. Morris Rabinowitz
31 Avenue M
Brooklyn, N.Y. 11216

    Morris Rabinowitz
31 Avenue N
Brooklyn, N.Y. 11216   20.____

KEY (CORRECT ANSWERS)

1.	D	11.	B
2.	B	12.	D
3.	C	13.	A
4.	A	14.	B
5.	B	15.	B
6.	C	16.	C
7.	D	17.	C
8.	A	18.	D
9.	B	19.	A
10.	D	20.	D

TEST 5

DIRECTIONS: In copying the addresses below from Column A to the same line in Column B, an Agent-in-Training made some errors. For Questions 1 through 5, if you find that the agent made an error in
only one line, mark your answer A;
only two lines, mark your answer B;
only three lines, mark your answer C;
all four lines, mark your answer D.

EXAMPLE

COLUMN A	COLUMN B
24 Third Avenue	24 Third Avenue
5 Lincoln Road	5 Lincoln Street
50 Central Park West	6 Central Park West
37-21 Queens Boulevard	21-37 Queens Boulevard

Since errors were made on only three lines, namely the second, third, and fourth, the CORRECT answer is C.
PRINT THE LETTER OF THE CORRECT ANSWER IN THE SPACE AT THE RIGHT.

COLUMN A   COLUMN B

1. 57-22 Springfield Boulevard   75-22 Springfield Boulevard   1._____
   94 Gun Hill Road   94 Gun Hill Avenue
   8 New Dorp Lane   8 New Drop Lane
   36 Bedford Avenue   36 Bedford Avenue

2. 538 Castle Hill Avenue   538 Castle Hill Avenue   2._____
   54-15 Beach Channel Drive   54-15 Beach Channel Drive
   21 Ralph Avenue   21 Ralph Avenue
   162 Madison Avenue   162 Morrison Avenue

3. 49 Thomas Street   49 Thomas Street   3._____
   27-21 Northern Blvd.   21-27 Northern Blvd.
   86 125th Street   86 125th Street
   872 Atlantic Ave.   872 Baltic Ave,

4. 261-17 Horace Harding Expwy.   261-17 Horace Harding Pkwy.   4._____
   191 Fordham Road   191 Fordham Road
   6 Victory Blvd.   6 Victoria Blvd.
   552 Oceanic Ave.   552 Ocean Ave.

5. 90-05 38th Avenue   90-05 36th Avenue   5._____
   19 Central Park West   19 Central Park East
   9281 Avenue X   9281 Avenue X
   22 West Farms Square   22 West Farms Square

124

KEY (CORRECT ANSWERS)

1. C
2. A
3. B
4. C
5. B

TEST 6

DIRECTIONS: For Questions 1 through 10, choose the letter in Column II next to the number which EXACTLY matches the number in Column I. *PRINT THE LETTER OF THE CORRECT ANSWER IN THE SPACE AT THE RIGHT.*

COLUMN I　　　　　　　　　　　COLUMN II

1. 14235
   - A. 13254
   - B. 12435
   - C. 13245
   - D. 14235

   1.____

2. 70698
   - A. 90768
   - B. 60978
   - C. 70698]
   - D. 70968

   2.____

3. 11698
   - A. 11689
   - B. 11986
   - C. 11968
   - D. 11698

   3.____

4. 50497
   - A. 50947
   - B. 50497
   - C. 50749
   - D. 54097

   4.____

5. 69635
   - A. 60653
   - B. 69630
   - C. 69365
   - D. 69635

   5.____

6. 1201022011
   - A. 1201022011
   - B. 1201020211
   - C. 1202012011
   - D. 1021202011

   6.____

7. 3893981389
   - A. 3893891389
   - B. 3983981389
   - C. 3983891389
   - D. 3893981389

   7.____

8. 4765476589
   - A. 4765476598
   - B. 4765476588
   - C. 4765476589
   - D. 4765746589

   8.____

9. 8679678938
    A. 8679687938
    B. 8679678938
    C. 8697678938
    D. 8678678938

    9.____

10. 6834836932
    A. 6834386932
    B. 6834836923
    C. 6843836932
    D. 6834836932

    10.____

Questions 11-15.

DIRECTIONS: For Questions 11 through 15, determine how many of the symbols in Column Z are exactly the same as the symbol in Column Y.
If none is exactly the same, answer A;
If only one symbol is exactly the same, answer B;
If two symbols are exactly the same, answer C;
If three symbols are exactly the same, answer D.

COLUMN Y	COLUMN Z	
11. A123B1266	A123B1366 A123B1266 A133B1366 A123B1266	11.____
12. CC28D3377	CD22D3377 CC38D3377 CC28C3377 CC28D2277	12.____
13. M21AB201X	M12AB201X M21AB201X M21AB201Y M21BA201X	13.____
14. PA383Y744	AP383Y744 PA338Y744 PA388Y744 PA383Y774	14.____
15. PB2Y8893	PB2Y8893 PB2Y8893 PB3Y8898 PB2Y8893	15.____

KEY (CORRECT ANSWERS)

1.	D	6.	A	11.	C
2.	C	7.	D	12.	A
3.	D	8.	C	13.	B
4.	B	9.	B	14.	A
5.	D	10.	D	15.	D

TELEMETRY AND COMMUNICATIONS

TABLE OF CONTENTS

	Page
Unit 1. Emergency Medical Services Communication System	1
Phases of an Emergency Medical Services Communication System	1
System Components	3
Radio Communications: Voice and Telemetry	4
Unit 2: Communications Regulations and Procedures	7
Federal Communications Commission	7
Protocols and Communication Procedures	7
Dispatch Procedures	7
Relaying Information to the Physician	11
Techniques	12
Glossary	14

TELEMETRY AND COMMUNICATIONS

Unit 1. Emergency Medical Services Communication System

An emergency medical services (EMS) communication system helps coordinate all groups and persons involved in emergency response and care. Such a communication system should be able to coordinate emergency medical services and resources during major emergencies and disasters, as well as during individual emergencies.

Phases of an Emergency Medical Services Communication System

Access and notification. How to notify the system when an emergency has occurred is an important aspect of EMS communications. Although telephones are the most common means of access available to the public, their usefulness is limited by their number and location and by the public's confusion as to whom to call for emergency assistance. The Yellow Pages of the telephone directory may offer a wide choice of emergency ambulance services; and, furthermore, operators may be unprepared to accept and refer a true emergency call.

The telephone is most useful in an emergency when the 911 universal access number is available. A bystander then can dial 911 from a home telephone or a callbox without needing correct change to notify the dispatch agency. The call goes to a communications coordination center (CCC) for police, fire, and medical emergencies. The emergency services operator in the center then notifies the appropriate emergency service.

Some communities also have free telephones or callboxes available on the highways for emergency use. When these highway phones or callboxes are properly connected for prompt access to an emergency services center, they make it easier for citizens to obtain emergency services.

The notification phase of emergency medical communications can be improved through public education. The public should know when emergency care is needed, whom to call to obtain appropriate aid, what to say in order to obtain advice, and what to expect in the way of a response.

Dispatch. Once the system has been notified, there must be a process through which appropriate emergency vehicles are selected and directed to the scene of the illness or injury. Vehicles can be dispatched by telephone (hard-line communication), radio, or a combination telephone/radio connection (phone patch).

It is easier and more economical to coordinate emergency services if the CCC dispatches police, fire, and emergency medical vehicles. Such centers can be organized to cover county or other regional areas, depending on local policy and municipal preferences. The CCC is especially helpful in coordinating emergency services during major emergencies and disasters.

Communication between dispatcher and emergency personnel. The Emergency Medical Technician-Paramedic (EMT-P) must have use of a radio at all times: en route to the emergency scene, at the scene, during transport to the hospital, and while returning to base after completing a call. The capability for rapid interconnection to medical advice should be at the fingertips of the dispatcher.

Dispatcher-to-paramedic communication is important for several reasons. It enables the dispatcher to give the EMT-P additional information while en route. It lets the dispatcher know where the emergency vehicle is and about how long it will be busy. It also allows redirection of the vehicle either when en route to the original destination or when traveling to the base station after completing a call. Further, it allows the EMT-P to request police or fire department assistance, additional ambulances, or additional emergency medical personnel.

Three-way communication among the paramedic physician and emergency department. Physicians, although usually hospital based, may be linked to the ambulance by a communication system in their cars, homes, or offices so that they can order advanced life-support procedures at the scene and during transport. In some States, specially trained nurses, operating under standing orders from physicians, can provide this consultation link with EMT-P's.

Communication with emergency department personnel allows the EMT-P to report the patient's condition and expected arrival time. This procedure gives the emergency department time to assemble necessary equipment and prepare for specific problems. In addition, such communication allows redirection of the EMS team to another facility if the original one does not have adequate treatment capabilities or bed space for a particular case.

Paramedics often use two-way radios to communicate with the physician, nurse, and emergency department. By means of the communication patching capabilities at the base station, the ambulance en route can communicate by mobile radio via phone patch or cross-frequency radio patch to someone at the accident scene. In addition, the ambulance en route or at the scene can communicate by mobile radio via patch to a physician at home or in a vehicle equipped with a telephone or citizens band (CB) radio.

Portable radio transmitter/receivers can be used for communications between the emergency scene and the hospital physician, usually via the ambulance relay. In this way, the EMT-P can receive instructions at the scene without having to return to the vehicle to use the mobile transmitter/receiver.

Communication among area hospitals. In a mass casualty situation, communication among area hospitals may be necessary to request blood or special supplies. In this phase, communication among hospitals may be by radio, telephone, or radio-telephone combination.

Communication links with support agencies. Communication with such support agencies as the fire and police departments and civil defense office or with crisis intervention teams can be accomplished through CCC's or through separate dispatch centers.

Although it is possible for dispatch centers to communicate by telephone, such connections may be disrupted or overloaded during a disaster. Therefore, dedicated telephone lines (lines used exclusively between two points) and/or a backup radio network should be available.

Coordination of other radio networks to be used in contingency planning. Private communication systems that normally are available during disasters include the. following:
- The Amateur Radio Public Service Corps (ARPSC) (Contact the ARPSC at the American Radio Relay League, Inc., Newington, Conn. 06111, for information on specific area groups.)

- The Radio Amateur Civil Emergency Service (RACES) (Contact local civil defense officials for information on community resources.)
- Business and municipal radio service systems (e.g., taxi-dispatching and trucking services)
- CB highway safety groups, such as REACT and NEAR (Some have been specially organized to respond to emergency situations through Channel 9, a designated emergency channel.

System Components

The hardware (components) used for medical communications varies considerably from system to system. A description of some of the coon hardware components of a communication network follows.

Base station transmitters and receivers. The base station is used for dispatch and coordination and, ideally, should be in contact with all other elements of the system. Directional antennas should be placed in the proper position to serve the desired area for radio coverage and at the same time not interfere with bordering service areas. The highest point is not necessarily the best location. Wire connections from base radio units to the dispatch center may be the most desirable method for reducing the number of airwave (radio) transmissions. This method allows greater use of radio channels and precludes interference to neighboring services. Transmission levels are limited by the Federal Communications Commission (FCC). The minimum usable levels for signal reception are limited by manmade noise such as automobile ignitions. A good antenna system can compensate partially for these limitations.

Base stations with multiple channels to provide automatic rotation to an open channel are available.

Mobile transmitter/receivers. Mobile transmitter/receivers are mounted in the emergency vehicles. They come in different power ranges. The antenna system, the power range of the transmitter/receiver, the kinds of buildings in the area, and terrain features determine the distance over which the units can transmit a signal. The reliability and radio transmission range can be insured substantially if the network of base stations and telephone interconnections is properly engineered.

Portable transmitter/receivers (two-way portable radios). Portable transmitter/receivers are handheld so that they can be carried outside the emergency vehicle by the EMT-P. Medical control physicians also carry portable transmitter/receivers for use when they cannot be reached immediately via the hospital-circuit radio.

Portable units usually have a power limitation of 5 watts. The signal of a handheld transmitter can be boosted to equal the range of a mobile unit by retransmission through the vehicle or base station for network connection. Portable transmitter/receivers can transmit and receive multiple frequencies.

Repeaters. Essentially repeaters are miniature base stations used to extend the transmitting and receiving range of a telemetry or voice communications system. Repeaters receive a signal on one frequency and retransmit it on a second frequency.

Repeaters may be fixed or mobile (carried in the emergency vehicle). Many systems employ both fixed and mobile repeaters. Repeaters are useful for extending the transmission range in hilly and mountainous areas, as well as for extending the range of portable transmitter/receivers. In both cases, the primary hardware (the patient-side radio) transmits the signal via the repeater in the vehicle; the signal then is retransmitted to the base station.

Remote console. The remote console is a control console connected to the base station by telephone lines. It allows use of the base station from another location such as a hospital emergency department.

The remote console both receives voice and telemetry signals from the field and transmits verbal messages back through the base station equipment. Remote consoles usually contain an amplifier and a speaker for incoming voice reception, a decoder for translating telemetry signals into an oscilloscope trace or readout, and a microphone for voice transmission.

Encoders and decoders. The dispatch center, ambulances, and hospitals in a communications system all share a small number of radio frequencies. Radio receivers on the same channel would be activated by every message if signals were not directed by the transmitting individual to the desired recipient. The encoder and decoder are the means by which incoming messages are directed to the desired recipient.

The encoder resembles a telephone dial. When a number is dialed, the encoder transmits a pulsed tone; the number of pulses equals the number dialed. All receivers operating on that frequency receive the pulsed tone. However, each receiver responds to only one pulsed code, which is its own three- or four-number address code. When this code reaches the receiver, the decoder opens the receiver's audio circuit. The encoder-decoder system does not prevent other users from listening in, but it does keep them from receiving unwanted messages.

Telephone. In addition to radio communications, many systems employ hard-line (telephone) backup to link fixed components of the system, such as hospitals, and fire and police services. Telephones can also be patched into radio transmission through the base, station ox through manual control at the CCC. This can allow communication between paramedics using radios in the field and physicians using their telephones at home. Although some telephone lines are already provided with amplifiers to insure a strong, undistorted signal, line clearing may be required at individual locations.

Radio Communications: Voice and Telemetry

Radio frequencies. Radio frequencies are designated in cycles per second. One cycle per second is defined as a hertz. The following abbreviations commonly are used:

hertz (Hz)	=	1 cycle per second
kilohertz (kHz)	=	1,000 cycles per second
megahertz (MHz)	=	1,000,000 cycles per second
gigahertz (GHz)	=	1,000,000,000 cycles per second

Radio waves are part of the electromagnetic frequency spectrum, which is assigned for different purposes. Different frequency bands have different properties. In general, higher frequency bands have a shorter transmission range but also have less signal distortion (interference and noise).

Emergency medical communications use both the very-high-frequency (VHF) band and the ultrahigh-frequency (UHF) band. The VHF band extends from about 30 to 175 MHz and is divided into a low band (30 to 50 MHz) and a high band (150 to 175 MHz). The low-band frequencies have ranges of up to 2,000 miles. However, these ranges are unpredictable because changes in atmospheric conditions sometimes produce "skip" interference that results in patchy losses in communication. The high-band frequencies are almost free of skip interference but have a shorter range. Specific frequencies in the VHF high band have been allocated by the FCC for emergency medical purposes.

The UHF band extends from 300 to 3,000 MHz. Most medical communications are in the 450- to 470-MHz range, which is free of skip interference and has little noise (signal distortion). The UHF band has better building penetration than VHF. The UHF band, however, has a shorter range than the VHF band, and UHF waves are absorbed more by environmental objects like trees and bushes.

Both VHF and UHF communication use frequency-modulated (FM) equipment rather than amplitude-modulated (AM) equipment. (Citizens band radios, in contrast, are AM.) There is less noise and interference with PM than with AN equipment.

The FCC assigns frequencies and has set aside frequencies on both bands for emergency, radio communications. A special set of 10 channels (paired frequencies) for EMS communication allows substantial channel space and great flexibility of use for voice and telemetry.

Biotelemetry. The term "biotelemetry" refers to a technique for measuring vital signs and transmitting them to a distant terminal. When the term "telemetry" is used in emergency medicine, it usually refers to transmission of an electrocardiogram (EKC) signal from the patient to a distant receiving station. In the EMS system, EKG telemetry is multiplexed on a normal voice channel using a subcarrier of 1,400 Hz, which may result in minor degradation of the voice transmission over the same channel. The hospital must be able to communicate with the paramedic while biotelemetry is in progress.

The EKG signal consists of low frequencies (100 Hz and less). Radio modulation techniques (in particular, FM) exhibit decreased responsiveness below 300 Hz. To avoid distortion, the EKG signals, are coded into a higher frequency using a reference audio tone of 1,400 Hz. The 1,400-Hz tone then is, modulated by the EKG signal for radio transmission. When the transmission reaches the distant terminals, it is amplified and demodulated to produce a signal voltage exactly like the original EKG signal.

Distortion of the EKG signal by extra spikes and waves is called "noise." This interference can result from the following conditions:

- Loose EKG electrodes
- Muscle tremors of the patient
- Sources of 60-cycle alternating current such as transformers, power lines, and electrical equipment

- Weakening of transmitter power due either to weak batteries or to transmission beyond base station range

Use of frequencies in a system. Assigned frequencies are used in different systems. In a simplex system, portable units can transmit in only one mode: (voice or telemetry) or receive only voice at any one time; such systems require only a single radio frequency. When a network uses two frequencies simultaneously, it is referred to as duplex. Another alternative is to combine, or multiplex, two or more signals so that they can be transmitted on one frequency at the same time.

Unit 2. Communications Regulations and Procedures

Federal Communications Commission

The FCC is a national regulatory and controlling agency. It assigns frequencies and licenses individuals and communications systems. In addition, the FCC establishes and enforces communications regulations.

To enforce its regulations, the FCC monitors frequencies and performs road checks. It also spot checks base stations and their records.

The FCC has offices throughout the country. All communication plans must be coordinated with these field offices. The EMT-P's should be familiar with FCC regulations.

Protocols and Communication Procedures

Standard operating, procedures (SOP's) are necessary to insure appropriate and efficient use of the medical communications system. Standard procedures eliminate unnecessary communication that could overload communication channels. By providing a structure, for essential communications, SOP's make it possible for the physician to quickly receive information about a patient's condition and rapidly transmit orders for the patient's care.

The possibility of misunderstood messages is reduced with SOP's. When these procedures involve coded messages, all persons using the communication system must understand the code and use it properly. These individuals include paramedics, dispatchers, physicians, emergency department staff, and others directly involved in radio communications.

Dispatch Procedures

The dispatcher gathers, information about the emergency, directs the appropriate vehicle to the scene, and advises the caller how to manage the emergency until help arrives. In addition, the dispatcher monitors and coordinates field communications. While performing these duties, the dispatcher must con form to FCC guidelines.

Information gathering. The dispatcher usually collects information by asking a short series of questions. When a call for an ambulance is received, the dispatcher records the necessary information as rapidly as possible. If tape recording equipment is available, a tape should be made of each call to serve as a backup record.

The dispatcher should obtain the following information:

- Phone number of the caller. This allows the dispatcher to contact the caller for more information (e.g., if the rescue team is unable to find the address and needs better directions). Asking for the caller's phone number also reduces nuisance calls because prank callers usually are reluctant to give their phone numbers. In addition, the phone number can help the dispatcher determine the caller's location if the caller (e.g., a traveler calling from the highway) is unfamiliar with the area.

- Name of the patient (if known). This information will help the rescue team to identify the patient.

- Exact location of the patient, including street name and number. The dispatcher must obtain the proper geographic designation (e.g., whether the street is East Maple or West Maple) and the community name, since nearby towns may have streets with the same names. If the call comes from a rural area, the dispatcher should establish landmarks, such as the nearest crossroad or business, or a water tower, antenna, or other easily identifiable landmark that will help the rescue team to orient itself.

- Nature of the patient's problem.

- Specific information about the patient's condition. (Is the patient conscious, breathing, bleeding badly, or in severe pain?)

- Whether the emergency is a highway accident. If it is the dispatcher should obtain the following additional information:

  -- Kinds of vehicles involved (cars, trucks, motorcycles, buses). If trucks are involved, the dispatcher should ask what they are carrying to determine the possibility of noxious fumes.

  -- Number of persons involved and extent of injuries. Even if the caller can only guess at this information, it can give the dispatcher an idea of the size of problem

  -- Known hazards, including traffic dangers, downed electrical wires, fire, submerged vehicles, and so forth. Information about these hazards allows the dispatcher to contact other agencies that will need to become involved, such as the utility department to deal with downed wires.

A special, preprinted form can help the dispatcher obtain all the necessary information and can provide a record of the call. Figure 14.2 provides a sample of such a form.

<u>Dispatch.</u> After the dispatchers receive the necessary information, they should ask callers to wait on the line. Dispatchers then must make several decisions.

- What is the nature of the problem? Is it life threatening?
- Are paramedics needed?
- Are support services needed (police, fire, heavy rescue)?
- Which crew(s) and vehicle(s) should respond? This decision will depend on the nature and
- location of the call and on which units are available. Thus, the dispatcher must know, the status of every area vehicle and crew in order to decide which to dispatch.

In order to make these decisions about medical emergencies, the dispatcher needs training in emergency medical care. The Division of Emergency Medical Services of the U.S. Department of Health, Education, and Welfare recommends that EMS dispatchers receive the same EMT training as the medical crews that they dispatch. The Department of Transportation has developed a special curriculum for dispatchers.

<u>Records.</u> Either the EMT-P or dispatcher or both should record key times for each call. This information should include the times that the call was received, the vehicle began the run, the crew arrived at the emergency scene, the crew left the scene, the patient reached the hospital, and the vehicle and crew were back in service.

10

Date _____   Log No. _____

TIMES

Call received _____ am./p.m.
Car out _____

Arrived at scene _____
Left scene _____
Arrived at hospital _____
Back in service _____
Patient's name _____
Address _____
City/town _____

PATIENT STATUS

Conscious _____
Breathing _____
Bleeding _____
Other _____

If vehicular accident:

Number and kinds of vehicles involved:

_____ Cars   _____ Trucks   _____ Buses   _____ Other

Number of persons injured _____

Extent of injuries _____

Are persons trapped? _____

Hazards:
  _____ Traffic   _____ Wires down   _____ Fire   _____ Hazardous car
  _____ Unstable vehicle   _____ Debris   _____ Submerged vehicle

Caller: Name _____ Phone No _____

Vehicle dispatched _____

Crew _____ Other units called _____

Figure 14.2. Sample dispatch record form.

Relaying Information to the Physician

Radio communications between the EMT-P's and their physician directors should be brief and accurate. To insure that information is transmitted in a consistent manner and that nothing significant is omitted, the paramedic should follow a standard procedure for relaying patient information. Such information should include:

- Patient's age and sex
- Vital signs
- Chief complaint
- Brief history of present illness
- Physical findings

    - State of consciousness
    - General appearance
    - Other pertinent observations

The following is an example of a concise, informative transmission for a patient in congestive heart failure:

We have a 53-year-old man with a pulse of 130 and regular, blood pressure 190/120, and respirations per minute. He is complaining of severe shortness of breath that wakened him from sleep and is worse when he is lying down. He has a history of high blood pressure and takes Diuril at home. He is alert but in considerable distress. He has rales and wheezes in both lung fields. We are sending you an EKG.

The above transmission takes less than 30 seconds but efficiently provides the physician with the information needed to rapidly dignose the problem and order appropriate treatment.

In contrast, the following dialogue can be considered:

EMT-P:	We have a patient with a pulse of 130, blood pressure of 190/120, and respirations of 30. We are sending you a strip.
Doctor:	Fine, but what's his problem?
EMT-P:	He's short of breath.
Doctor:	How long has this been going on?
EMT-P:	Just a minute. (Pause) He says it woke him up from sleep about an hour ago.
Doctor:	Does he have any underlying medical problems?
EMT-P:	He takes medicine for hypertension.
Doctor:	Is he in any distress?
EMT-P:	Yes, he's having a hard time breathing.
Doctor:	What do his lungs sound like?
EMT-P:	Just a minute. (Pause) He has rales and wheezes all over.

This type of communication obviously is less efficient. It wastes time and annoys and frustrates everyone. Information should be gathered at the scene and organized clearly in the EMT-P's mind before the physician is contacted. The reporting procedure can be written on a card posted in the vehicle or on the transmitter, so the paramedic can refer to it when reporting in.

Techniques

Radio communications equipment varies from manufacturer to manufacturer. Therefore, the directions in this section are general, rather than specific. These directions must be supplemented with more specific instructions for the equipment in use.

<u>Use of a mobile transmitter/receiver.</u> The EMT-P should:
- Turn unit on
- Adjust squelch
- Listen to be sure airways are free of other communications
- Hold microphone far enough from the mouth to avoid exhaled air noise
- Push the push-to-talk button, and pause before speaking
- When calling another unit, use its call letters first, and the sender's second
- Follow these guidelines when using the radio

    -- Use an understandable rate of speech
    -- Do not talk too loudly -- Do not hesitate
    -- Articulate clearly
    -- Speak with good voice quality
    -- Avoid dialect or slang
    -- Do not show emotion
    -- Avoid vocalized pauses (such as "urn," "uh," "hmm") -- Use proper English
    -- Avoid excessive transmission

- Use the call sign to let others know the transmission is completed

<u>Use of a portable transmitter/receiver.</u> Use of a portable transmitter/receiver is similar to use of a mobile transmitter/receiver. Since the antenna on the portable unit is not fixed in place, however, it must be kept vertical while in use so that the signal can be properly transmitted to the vehicle. From the vehicle, the signal can be transmitted to the base station.

<u>Use of a digital encoder.</u> The EMT-P should:

- Turn unit on
- Adjust squelch
- Listen to be sure airways are free of other communication
- Select address code to be dialed
- Dial selected numbers
- Hold microphone far enough from the mouth to avoid exhaled air noise
- Push the push-to-talk button, and pause before speaking
- Call dialed unit
- Use the call sign to let others know the transmission is completed

<u>Transmission of patient assessment information and telemetry.</u> The EMT-P should:

- Turn unit on
- Adjust squelch
- Listen to be sure airways are free of other communication
- Hold microphone far enough from the mouth to avoid exhaled air noise
- Push the push-to-talk button and pause before speaking

- Call physician either directly or through a relay system
- Connect or attach electrodes to telemetry transmitter
- Follow local procedure for relaying patient assessment information
- Activate telemetry transmitter for the minimum amount of time required by the receiving physician (approximately 15 seconds)
- Verify physician's reception and quality of transmission

GLOSSARY

dispatch: To transmit calls to emergency medical, services and to direct emergency vehicles, equipment, and personnel to the scene of a medical emergency.

duplex: A radio communications system employing more than one frequency.

Federal Communications Commission (FCC): The Federal regulatory agency that assigns radio frequencies and licenses individuals and communications systems.

frequency: The number of periodic waves per unit of time; radio waves are expressed in cycles per second.

frequency modulation: A method of converting an analog signal, such as an electrocardiogram, into a tone of varying pitch that can be transmitted over the radio.

gigahertz (GHz): A unit of frequency measurement equaling 1 billion Hz; indicates frequencies of 1 billion cycles per second.

hertz (Hz): A unit of frequency measurement; 1 Hz equals 1 cycle per second.

kilohertz (kHz): A unit equaling 1,000 Hz; it indicates frequencies of 1,000 cycles per second.

megahertz (MHz): A unit equaling 1 million Hz; indicates frequencies of 1 million cycles per second.

multiplex: In a radio communications system, a method by which simultaneous transmission and reception of voice and electrocardiogram signals can be achieved over a single frequency.

noise: Extra spikes, waves, and complexes in the EKG signal caused by various conditions such as muscle tremor, 60-cycle alternating-current interference, improperly attached electrodes, and out-of-range transmission.

patch: Connection of telephone line and radio communication systems making it possible for police, fire department, and medical personnel to communicate directly with each other by dialing into a special phone.

repeater: A miniature transmitter that picks up a radio signal and rebroadcasts it, thus extending the range of a radio communications system.

response time: The length of time required for the emergency medical services team to arrive at the scene of an emergency after receiving a call for help.

simplex: A communications system that can transmit only in one mode at a time, or receive voice transmissions only.

telemetry: The use of telecommunications for automatically indicating a recorded measurement at a location different from the measuring instrument, such as an electrocardiogram sent from an ambulance and received at a hospital.

UHF band: The ultrahigh-frequency band; refers to the portion of the radio frequency spectrum between 300 and 3,000 MHz.

VHF band: The very-high-frequency band; refers to the portion of the radio frequency spectrum between 30 and 150 MHz.

ELECTRICAL TERMS AND FORMULAS

CONTENTS

	Page
TERMS	1
Agonic ...... Dielectric	1
Diode ...... Lead	2
Line of Force ...... Resistor	3
Retentivity ...... Wattmeter	4
FORMULAS	4
Ohm's Law for D-C Circuits	4
Resistors in Series	4
Resistors in Parallel	4
R-L Circuit Time Constant	5
R-C Circuit Time Constant	5
Comparison of Units in Electric and Magnetic Circuits	5
Capacitors in Series	5
Capacitors in Parallel	5
Capacitive Reactance	5
Impedance in an R-C Circuit (Series)	5
Inductors in Series	5
Inductors in Parallel	5
Inductive Reactance	5
Q of a Coil	5
Impedance of an R-L Circuit (Series)	5
Impedance with R, C, and L in Series	5
Parallel Circuit Impedance	5
Sine-Wave Voltage Relationships	5
Power in A-C Circuit	6
Transformers	6
Three-Phase Voltage and Current Relationships	6
GREEK ALPHABET	7
Alpha ...... Omega	7
COMMON ABBREVIATIONS AND LETTER SYMBOLS	8
Alternating Current (noun) ...... Watt	8

ELECTRICAL TERMS AND FORMULAS

Terms

AGONIC.—An imaginary line of the earth's surface passing through points where the magnetic declination is 0°; that is, points where the compass points to true north.

AMMETER.—An instrument for measuring the amount of electron flow in amperes.

AMPERE.—The basic unit of electrical current.

AMPERE-TURN.—The magnetizing force produced by a current of one ampere flowing through a coil of one turn.

AMPLIDYNE.—A rotary magnetic or dynamoelectric amplifier used in servomechanism and control applications.

AMPLIFICATION.—The process of increasing the strength (current, power, or voltage) of a signal.

AMPLIFIER.—A device used to increase the signal voltage, current, or power, generally composed of a vacuum tube and associated circuit called a stage. It may contain several stages in order to obtain a desired gain.

AMPLITUDE.—The maximum instantaneous value of an alternating voltage or current, measured in either the positive or negative direction.

ARC.—A flash caused by an electric current ionizing a gas or vapor.

ARMATURE.—The rotating part of an electric motor or generator. The moving part of a relay or vibrator.

ATTENUATOR.—A network of resistors used to reduce voltage, current, or power delivered to a load.

AUTOTRANSFORMER.—A transformer in which the primary and secondary are connected together in one winding.

BATTERY.—Two or more primary or secondary cells connected together electrically. The term does not apply to a single cell.

BREAKER POINTS.—Metal contacts that open and close a circuit at timed intervals.

BRIDGE CIRCUIT.—The electrical bridge circuit is a term referring to any one of a variety of electric circuit networks, one branch of which, the "bridge" proper, connects two points of equal potential and hence carries no current when the circuit is properly adjusted or balanced.

BRUSH.—The conducting material, usually a block of carbon, bearing against the commutator or sliprings through which the current flows in or out.

BUS BAR.—A primary power distribution point connected to the main power source.

CAPACITOR.—Two electrodes or sets of electrodes in the form of plates, separated from each other by an insulating material called the dielectric.

CHOKE COIL.—A coil of low ohmic resistance and high impedance to alternating current.

CIRCUIT.—The complete path of an electric current.

CIRCUIT BREAKER.—An electromagnetic or thermal device that opens a circuit when the current in the circuit exceeds a predetermined amount. Circuit breakers can be reset.

CIRCULAR MIL.—An area equal to that of a circle with a diameter of 0.001 inch. It is used for measuring the cross section of wires.

COAXIAL CABLE.—A transmission line consisting of two conductors concentric with and insulated from each other.

COMMUTATOR.—The copper segments on the armature of a motor or generator. It is cylindrical in shape and is used to pass power into or from the brushes. It is a switching device.

CONDUCTANCE.—The ability of a material to conduct or carry an electric current. It is the reciprocal of the resistance of the material, and is expressed in mhos.

CONDUCTIVITY.—The ease with which a substance transmits electricity.

CONDUCTOR.—Any material suitable for carrying electric current.

CORE.—A magnetic material that affords an easy path for magnetic flux lines in a coil.

COUNTER E.M.F.—Counter electromotive force; an e.m.f. induced in a coil or armature that opposes the applied voltage.

CURRENT LIMITER.—A protective device similar to a fuse, usually used in high amperage circuits.

CYCLE.—One complete positive and one complete negative alternation of a current or voltage.

DIELECTRIC.—An insulator; a term that refers to the insulating material between the plates of a capacitor.

ELECTRICAL TERMS AND FORMULAS

DIODE.—Vacuum tube—a two element tube that contains a cathode and plate; semiconductor—a material of either germanium or silicon that is manufactured to allow current to flow in only one direction. Diodes are used as rectifiers and detectors.

DIRECT CURRENT.—An electric current that flows in one direction only.

EDDY CURRENT.—Induced circulating currents in a conducting material that are caused by a varying magnetic field.

EFFICIENCY.—The ratio of output power to input power, generally expressed as a percentage.

ELECTROLYTE.—A solution of a substance which is capable of conducting electricity. An electrolyte may be in the form of either a liquid or a paste.

ELECTROMAGNET.—A magnet made by passing current through a coil of wire wound on a soft iron core.

ELECTROMOTIVE FORCE (e.m.f.).—The force that produces an electric current in a circuit.

ELECTRON.—A negatively charged particle of matter.

ENERGY.—The ability or capacity to do work.

FARAD.—The unit of capacitance.

FEEDBACK.—A transfer of energy from the output circuit of a device back to its input.

FIELD.—The space containing electric or magnetic lines of force.

FIELD WINDING.—The coil used to provide the magnetizing force in motors and generators.

FLUX FIELD.—All electric or magnetic lines of force in a given region.

FREE ELECTRONS.—Electrons which are loosely held and consequently tend to move at random among the atoms of the material.

FREQUENCY.—The number of complete cycles per second existing in any form of wave motion; such as the number of cycles per second of an alternating current.

FULL-WAVE RECTIFIER CIRCUIT.—A circuit which utilizes both the positive and the negative alternations of an alternating current to produce a direct current.

FUSE.—A protective device inserted in series with a circuit. It contains a metal that will melt or break when current is increased beyond a specific value for a definite period of time.

GAIN.—The ratio of the output power, voltage, or current to the input power, voltage, or current, respectively.

GALVANOMETER.—An instrument used to measure small d-c currents.

GENERATOR.—A machine that converts mechanical energy into electrical energy.

GROUND.—A metallic connection with the earth to establish ground potential. Also, a common return to a point of zero potential. The chassis of a receiver or a transmitter is sometimes the common return, and therefore the ground of the unit.

HENRY.—The basic unit of inductance.

HORSEPOWER.—The English unit of power, equal to work done at the rate of 550 foot-pounds per second. Equal to 746 watts of electrical power.

HYSTERESIS.—A lagging of the magnetic flux in a magnetic material behind the magnetizing force which is producing it.

IMPEDANCE.—The total opposition offered to the flow of an alternating current. It may consist of any combination of resistance, inductive reactance, and capacitive reactance.

INDUCTANCE.—The property of a circuit which tends to oppose a change in the existing current.

INDUCTION.—The act or process of producing voltage by the relative motion of a magnetic field across a conductor.

INDUCTIVE REACTANCE.—The opposition to the flow of alternating or pulsating current caused by the inductance of a circuit. It is measured in ohms.

INPHASE.—Applied to the condition that exists when two waves of the same frequency pass through their maximum and minimum values of like polarity at the same instant.

INVERSELY.—Inverted or reversed in position or relationship.

ISOGONIC LINE.—An imaginary line drawn through points on the earth's surface where the magnetic deviation is equal.

JOULE.—A unit of energy or work. A joule of energy is liberated by one ampere flowing for one second through a resistance of one ohm.

KILO.—A prefix meaning 1,000.

LAG.—The amount one wave is behind another in time; expressed in electrical degrees.

LAMINATED CORE.—A core built up from thin sheets of metal and used in transformers and relays.

LEAD.—The opposite of LAG. Also, a wire or connection.

ELECTRICAL TERMS AND FORMULAS

LINE OF FORCE.—A line in an electric or magnetic field that shows the direction of the force.

LOAD.—The power that is being delivered by any power producing device. The equipment that uses the power from the power producing device.

MAGNETIC AMPLIFIER.—A saturable reactor type device that is used in a circuit to amplify or control.

MAGNETIC CIRCUIT.—The complete path of magnetic lines of force.

MAGNETIC FIELD.—The space in which a magnetic force exists.

MAGNETIC FLUX.—The total number of lines of force issuing from a pole of a magnet.

MAGNETIZE.—To convert a material into a magnet by causing the molecules to rearrange.

MAGNETO.—A generator which produces alternating current and has a permanent magnet as its field.

MEGGER.—A test instrument used to measure insulation resistance and other high resistances. It is a portable hand operated d-c generator used as an ohmmeter.

MEGOHM.—A million ohms.

MICRO.—A prefix meaning one-millionth.

MILLI.—A prefix meaning one-thousandth.

MILLIAMMETER.—An ammeter that measures current in thousandths of an ampere.

MOTOR-GENERATOR.—A motor and a generator with a common shaft used to convert line voltages to other voltages or frequencies.

MUTUAL INDUCTANCE.—A circuit property existing when the relative position of two inductors causes the magnetic lines of force from one to link with the turns of the other.

NEGATIVE CHARGE.—The electrical charge carried by a body which has an excess of electrons.

NEUTRON.—A particle having the weight of a proton but carrying no electric charge. It is located in the nucleus of an atom.

NUCLEUS.—The central part of an atom that is mainly comprised of protons and neutrons. It is the part of the atom that has the most mass.

NULL.—Zero.

OHM.—The unit of electrical resistance.

OHMMETER.—An instrument for directly measuring resistance in ohms.

OVERLOAD.—A load greater than the rated load of an electrical device.

PERMALLOY.—An alloy of nickel and iron having an abnormally high magnetic permeability.

PERMEABILITY.—A measure of the ease with which magnetic lines of force can flow through a material as compared to air.

PHASE DIFFERENCE.—The time in electrical degrees by which one wave leads or lags another.

POLARITY.—The character of having magnetic poles, or electric charges.

POLE.—The section of a magnet where the flux lines are concentrated; also where they enter and leave the magnet. An electrode of a battery.

POLYPHASE.—A circuit that utilizes more than one phase of alternating current.

POSITIVE CHARGE.—The electrical charge carried by a body which has become deficient in electrons.

POTENTIAL.—The amount of charge held by a body as compared to another point or body. Usually measured in volts.

POTENTIOMETER.—A variable voltage divider; a resistor which has a variable contact arm so that any portion of the potential applied between its ends may be selected.

POWER.—The rate of doing work or the rate of expending energy. The unit of electrical power is the watt.

POWER FACTOR.—The ratio of the actual power of an alternating or pulsating current, as measured by a wattmeter, to the apparent power, as indicated by ammeter and voltmeter readings. The power factor of an inductor, capacitor, or insulator is an expression of their losses.

PRIME MOVER.—The source of mechanical power used to drive the rotor of a generator.

PROTON.—A positively charged particle in the nucleus of an atom.

RATIO.—The value obtained by dividing one number by another, indicating their relative proportions.

REACTANCE.—The opposition offered to the flow of an alternating current by the inductance, capacitance, or both, in any circuit.

RECTIFIERS.—Devices used to change alternating current to unidirectional current. These may be vacuum tubes, semiconductors such as germanium and silicon, and dry-disk rectifiers such as selenium and copper-oxide.

RELAY.—An electromechanical switching device that can be used as a remote control.

RELUCTANCE.—A measure of the opposition that a material offers to magnetic lines of force.

RESISTANCE.—The opposition to the flow of current caused by the nature and physical dimensions of a conductor.

RESISTOR.—A circuit element whose chief characteristic is resistance; used to oppose the flow of current.

ELECTRICAL TERMS AND FORMULAS

RETENTIVITY.—The measure of the ability of a material to hold its magnetism.

RHEOSTAT.—A variable resistor.

SATURABLE REACTOR.—A control device that uses a small d-c current to control a large a-c current by controlling core flux density.

SATURATION.—The condition existing in any circuit when an increase in the driving signal produces no further change in the resultant effect.

SELF-INDUCTION.—The process by which a circuit induces an e.m.f. into itself by its own magnetic field.

SERIES-WOUND.—A motor or generator in which the armature is wired in series with the field winding.

SERVO.—A device used to convert a small movement into one of greater movement or force.

SERVOMECHANISM.—A closed-loop system that produces a force to position an object in accordance with the information that originates at the input.

SOLENOID.—An electromagnetic coil that contains a movable plunger.

SPACE CHARGE.—The cloud of electrons existing in the space between the cathode and plate in a vacuum tube, formed by the electrons emitted from the cathode in excess of those immediately attracted to the plate.

SPECIFIC GRAVITY—The ratio between the density of a substance and that of pure water, at a given temperature.

SYNCHROSCOPE—An instrument used to indicate a difference in frequency between two a-c sources.

SYNCHRO SYSTEM.—An electrical system that gives remote indications or control by means of self-synchronizing motors.

TACHOMETER.—An instrument for indicating revolutions per minute.

TERTIARY WINDING.—A third winding on a transformer or magnetic amplifier that is used as a second control winding.

THERMISTOR.—A resistor that is used to compensate for temperature variations in a circuit.

THERMOCOUPLE.—A junction of two dissimilar metals that produces a voltage when heated.

TORQUE.—The turning effort or twist which a shaft sustains when transmitting power.

TRANSFORMER.—A device composed of two or more coils, linked by magnetic lines of force, used to transfer energy from one circuit to another.

TRANSMISSION LINES.—Any conductor or system of conductors used to carry electrical energy from its source to a load.

VARS.—Abbreviation for volt-ampere, reactive.

VECTOR.—A line used to represent both direction and magnitude.

VOLT.—The unit of electrical potential.

VOLTMETER.—An instrument designed to measure a difference in electrical potential, in volts.

WATT.—The unit of electrical power.

WATTMETER.—An instrument for measuring electrical power in watts.

Formulas

Ohm's Law for d-c Circuits

$$I = \frac{E}{R} = \frac{P}{E} = \sqrt{\frac{P}{R}}$$

$$R = \frac{E}{I} = \frac{P}{I^2} = \frac{E^2}{P}$$

$$E = IR = \frac{P}{I} = \sqrt{PR}$$

$$P = EI = \frac{E^2}{R} = I^2 R$$

Resistors in Series

$$R_T = R_1 + R_2 \ldots$$

Resistors in Parallel
Two resistors

$$R_T = \frac{R_1 R_2}{R_1 + R_2}$$

More than two

$$\frac{1}{R_T} = \frac{1}{R_1} + \frac{1}{R_2} + \frac{1}{R_3}$$

ELECTRICAL TERMS AND FORMULAS

R-L Circuit Time Constant equals

$\dfrac{L \text{ (in henrys)}}{R \text{ (in ohms)}} = t$ (in seconds), or

$\dfrac{L \text{ (in microhenrys)}}{R \text{ (in ohms)}} = t$ (in microseconds)

R-C Circuit Time Constant equals
R (ohms) × C (farads) = t (seconds)
R (megohms) × C (microfarads) = t (seconds)
R (ohms) × C (microfarads) = t (microseconds)
R (megohms) × C (micromicrofrads = t (microseconds)

Comparison of Units in Electric and Magnetic Circuits.

	Electric circuit	Magnetic circuit
Force	Volt, E or e.m.f.	Gilberts, F, or m.m.f.
Flow	Ampere, I	Flux, Φ, in maxwells
Opposition	Ohms, R	Reluctance, R
Law	Ohm's law, $I = \dfrac{E}{R}$	Rowland's law $\Phi = \dfrac{F}{R}$
Intensity of force	Volts per cm. of length	$H = \dfrac{1.257IN}{L}$, gilberts per centimeter of length
Density	Current density—for example, amperes per cm^2.	Flux density—for example, lines per cm^2., or gausses

Capacitors in Series
Two capacitors

$$C_T = \dfrac{C_1 C_2}{C_1 + C_2}$$

More than two

$$\dfrac{1}{C_T} = \dfrac{1}{C_1} + \dfrac{1}{C_2} + \dfrac{1}{C_3}\ldots$$

Capacitors in Parallel

$$C_T = C_1 + C_2\ldots$$

Capacitive Reactance

$$X_c = \dfrac{1}{2\pi f C}$$

Impedance in an R-C Circuit (Series)

$$Z = \sqrt{R^2 + X_c^2}$$

Inductors in Series

$L_T = L_1 + L_2 \ldots$ (No coupling between coils)

Inductors in Parallel
Two inductors

$L_T = \dfrac{L_1 L_2}{L_1 + L_2}$ (No coupling between coils)

More than two

$\dfrac{1}{L_T} = \dfrac{1}{L_1} + \dfrac{1}{L_2} + \dfrac{1}{L_3} \ldots$ (No coupling between coils)

Inductive Reactance

$$X_L = 2\pi f L$$

Q of a Coil

$$Q = \dfrac{X_L}{R}$$

Impedance of an R-L Circuit (series)

$$Z = \sqrt{R^2 + X_L^2}$$

Impedance with R, C, and L in Series

$$Z = \sqrt{R^2 + (X_L - X_C)^2}$$

Parallel Circuit Impedance

$$Z = \dfrac{Z_1 Z_2}{Z_1 + Z_2}$$

Sine-Wave Voltage Relationships
Average value

$$E_{ave} = \dfrac{2}{\pi} \times E_{max} = 0.637 E_{max}$$

ELECTRICAL TERMS AND FORMULAS

Effective or r.m.s. value

$$E_{eff} = \frac{E_{max}}{\sqrt{2}} = \frac{E_{max}}{1.414} = 0.707 E_{max} = 1.11 E_{ave}$$

Maximum value

$$E_{max} = \sqrt{2} E_{eff} = 1.414 E_{eff} = 1.57 E_{ave}$$

Voltage in an a-c circuit

$$E = IZ = \frac{P}{I \times P.F.}$$

Current in an a-c circuit

$$I = \frac{E}{Z} = \frac{P}{E \times P.F.}$$

Power in A-C Circuit
  Apparent power = EI
  True power

$$P = EI \cos \theta = EI \times P.F.$$

Power factor

$$P.F. = \frac{P}{EI} = \cos \theta$$

$$\cos \theta = \frac{true\ power}{apparent\ power}$$

Transformers
  Voltage relationship

$$\frac{E}{E} = \frac{N}{N} \quad \text{or} \quad E = E \times \frac{N}{N}$$

Current relationship

$$\frac{I_p}{I_s} = \frac{N_s}{N_p}$$

Induced voltage

$$E_{eff} = 4.44\, BAfN 10^{-8}$$

Turns ratio equals

$$\frac{N_p}{N_s} = \sqrt{\frac{Z_p}{Z_s}}$$

Secondary current

$$I_s = I_p \frac{N_p}{N_s}$$

Secondary voltage

$$E_s = E_p \frac{N_s}{N_p}$$

Three Phase Voltage and Current Relationships
With wye connected windings

$$E_{line} = 1.732 E_{coil} = \sqrt{3} E_{coil}$$

$$I_{line} = I_{coil}$$

With delta connected windings

$$E_{line} = E_{coil}$$

$$I_{line} = 1.732 I_{coil}$$

With wye or delta connected winding

$$P_{coil} = E_{coil} I_{coil}$$

$$P_t = 3 P_{coil}$$

$$P_t = 1.732 E_{line} I_{line}$$

(To convert to true power multiply by $\cos \theta$)

Synchronous Speed of Motor

$$r.p.m. = \frac{120 \times frequency}{number\ of\ poles}$$

GREEK ALPHABET

Name	Capital	Lower Case	Designates
Alpha	A	α	Angles.
Beta	B	β	Angles, flux density.
Gamma	Γ	γ	Conductivity.
Delta	Δ	δ	Variation of a quantity, increment.
Epsilon	E	ϵ	Base of natural logarithms (2.71828).
Zeta	Z	ζ	Impedance, coefficients, coordinates.
Eta	H	η	Hysteresis coefficient, efficiency, magnetizing force.
Theta	Θ	θ	Phase angle.
Iota	I	ι	
Kappa	K	κ	Dielectric constant, coupling coefficient, susceptibility.
Lambda	Λ	λ	Wavelength.
Mu	M	μ	Permeability, micro, amplification factor.
Nu	N	ν	Reluctivity.
Xi	Ξ	ξ	
Omicron	O	o	
Pi	Π	π	3.1416
Rho	P	ρ	Resistivity.
Sigma	Σ	σ	
Tau	T	τ	Time constant, time-phase displacement.
Upsilon	Υ	υ	
Phi	Φ	φ	Angles, magnetic flux.
Chi	X	χ	
Psi	Ψ	ψ	Dielectric flux, phase difference.
Omega	Ω	ω	Ohms (capital), angular velocity ($2\pi f$).

COMMON ABBREVIATIONS AND LETTER SYMBOLS

Term	Abbreviation or Symbol
alternating current (noun)	a.c.
alternating-current (adj.)	a-c
ampere	a.
area	A
audiofrequency (noun)	AF
audiofrequency (adj.)	A-F
capacitance	C
capacitive reactance	X_C
centimeter	cm.
conductance	G
coulomb	Q
counterelectromotive force	c.e.m.f.
current (d-c or r.m.s. value)	I
current (instantaneous value)	i
cycles per second	c.p.s.
dielectric constant	K, k
difference in potential (d-c or r.m.s. value)	E
difference in potential (instantaneous value)	e
direct current (noun)	d.c.
direct-current (adj.)	d-c
electromotive force	e.m.f.
frequency	f
henry	h.
horsepower	hp.
impedance	Z
inductance	L
inductive reactance	X_L
kilovolt	kv.
kilovolt-ampere	kv.-a.
kilowatt	kw.
kilowatt-hour	kw.-hr.
magnetic field intensity	H
magnetomotive force	m.m.f.
megohm	M
microampere	μa.
microfarad	μf.
microhenry	μh.
micromicrofarad	$\mu\mu$f.
microvolt	μv.
milliampere	ma.
millihenry	mh.
milliwatt	mw.
mutual inductance	M
power	P
resistance	R
revolutions per minute	r.p.m.
root mean square	r.m.s.
time	t
torque	T
volt	v.
watt	w.

www.ingramcontent.com/pod-product-compliance
Lightning Source LLC
Chambersburg PA
CBHW082046300426
44117CB00015B/2627